Priscilla, Ellie's mother, said,

"The idea of Ellie 'turning on' at age fourteen was so remote that there seemed to be no reason to even consider it."

Ellie said,

"After I took those whites, all of a sudden I just started meeting all the dopers in school," . . . and . . . "When I got to Frisco—oh boy—was I dropping acid, like every day."

There is a way back—and this book tells the hows and whys and whens.

RETURN FROM A FAR COUNTRY

RETURN
FROM
A
FAR COUNTRY

by Holly Lee Vecchio

w

THE WESTMINSTER PRESS
Philadelphia

To my loving parents,
Emil R. and Elizabeth G. Vecchio
because they never kept score

CONTENTS

ACKNOWLEDGMENTS

OBVIOUSLY, this book would not have been possible without the openhearted cooperation and self-giving of the "Bernard" family. To "Ellie" and "Priscilla" and "Bob" go my very earnest thanks and my strong best wishes for the future.

There are others to whom one owes appreciation: Rev. James A. Glyer, for his interviews and general helpfulness; Mrs. Mary Matheson, a writer of extraordinary imagery, for so faithfully and helpfully reading and evaluating this material week after week; Mr. Norman Langston, Mr. Rod Fridlund, and Miss Lois McClure, of Westminster-Bethany Book Store in Los Angeles, for putting me in contact with a publisher; and Dr. Dean

Collins, Mr. Alfred Bettridge, and various other office members of that remarkable organization, the American Bible Society, Western and Pacific Region, for their kindness in understanding my need to work an irregular schedule.

Also, for the many lovely friends who have been so encouraging in so many, many thoughtful ways, I am truly grateful.

H.L.V.

The younger son gathered all he had and took his journey into a far country, and there he squandered his property in loose living.—*Luke 15:13.*

PROLOGUE

"THE GUY'S GUTS just ache. It's his daughter's sixteenth birthday, and he doesn't know if she's dead or alive."

"He" is Bob Bernard, father of Ellie Bernard, who at the time of the comment was a runaway teen and a drug addict. The remark was made by a pastor friend of the family.

Ironically, Ellie, with traces of hippie dialect still seasoning her speech, now says: "I think the time I felt loneliest was on my birthday, when I turned sixteen. And it was funny, 'cause like this bunch of people had a birthday party for me. And it was a funny feeling: I felt so lonely for my parents. But I felt like, well, somebody really loves me—y'know?—these people that were doing this for me. It was really emotional. But I kept thinking, 'Wow! Wouldn't it be beautiful if these were my parents doing this for me.' "

Two parents, aching to have their child safely home; one child, yearning to be safely home.

If this book has a message, it is somewhere in that paradox. To runaway youngsters: You *can* go home! To anxious parents: Kids *do* come back!

As we review Ellie's history, we do not presume to draw any conclusions about what kinds of teens go the runaway and drug route, or what kind of homelife produces the delinquent. Obviously, if the cause, or the virus, so to speak, could be isolated, we'd be able to produce the vaccine.

But the fact is, we have no mass preventative. Thousands of American teen-agers from all varieties of homes have sliced themselves away from their families. Many of them are confused or frightened, or hurt or lonely; further, many of their parents are anguished and fearful, and haunted by guilt.

If healing is to take place, both the youngsters and their parents need to be surrounded by the kind of reassurance and support that will enable them to make their mistakes without fear of permanent alienation from each other, and without the judgment of other relatives, or friends, or society in general. Otherwise, how can either child or parent bear to be honest about his own mistakes? If love has any meaning at all, the love that most of us would claim as the center of our faith, then it ought to work at this most primary level: it ought to enable us to forgive each other *within the family*.

We hope some of the experiences of the Bernard

family will have some redemptive meaning for other families. The Bernard family is very real, though their names are changed to protect them, particularly "Ellie," from those who might choose not to be forbearing. Names of all other persons are also fictionalized.

1

"WHERE DID
WE GO WRONG?"

AT THIRTY-SEVEN, Priscilla Bernard, Ellie's mother, is a very articulate, soft-spoken, gentle sort of person who hardly looks old enough to be the mother of a teen. She is an accomplished pianist and seems to have passed her musical interest on to her daughter, who plays the guitar, composes folk songs, and sings remarkably well. Though Priscilla seems innately shy, she is able to be surprisingly open about her daughter's runaway experience. She appears to be equally honest with strangers who ask, with her husband, and with herself.

Bob Bernard is also younger-looking than his forty-two years. Like Priscilla, he is also very articulate, though he is very deliberate in his speech. He appears to be quite conscious of his role as protector of his family, and seems to want to cover the bases without becoming dictatorial. He too is able to speak freely and honestly about the disaster that hit their family. He could, for instance, in front of Ellie speak of his own tears, shed when she first left home.

There are two other children in the family, sons much younger than Ellie.

The Bernards have searched every pocket of their souls to find reasons for the crisis that rattled their household: Where did they go wrong?

BOB: At first we tried to blame the trouble on the crowd Ellie was going with. And we blamed it for a while on the brief move we made from southern California to central California, because there she got in with older kids.

PRISCILLA: We think now there are things that go back to Ellie's childhood that we didn't recognize at the time as indicators of future problems. She was always highly emotional and very dependent on other people, especially on other people her own age. Also, very early, she found dramatic ways of gaining our full parental attention.

BOB: Right. At about age two she used to have these temper tantrums. She'd hold her breath until she passed out. Just hold her breath, and change color, and drop on the floor. Then as she got older, four or five years old, she developed tremendous nosebleeds.

PRISCILLA: She got a huge amount of attention during one of them, because they were really like gushers. Eventually we became suspicious that they were self-induced. It dawned on us that they always came when we were scolding her, or when she'd had an argument with a friend, or when she felt the need for some special consideration.

BOB: Having rushed her to the doctor again, we asked him if it were possible that she was causing them herself. He said to her, "Ellie, how do you start your nosebleeds?" And she rubbed her nose with her finger and the blood gushed. What she had done was merely wear down the membrane.

PRISCILLA: This was still at a time when she was the only child and had all the attention we could possibly give her. She's always had a tremendous need for attention.

BOB: And she was always bored. She always had to have somebody doing something with her. If Priscilla wasn't reading to her, or playing games with her, she had to have other children around her.

PRISCILLA: She needed the approval of the group all the time. This may have been a contributing factor to her later troubles. For instance, as she got older it was impressed on her in school that she was brighter than the average. And there seemed to be this trend among educators: the idea that you question, and challenge, and question and challenge everything. About the time she was in eighth grade this became a big thing with Ellie, to challenge all the standards. It was a sign of superior intelligence.

BOB: And a way to gain approval.

PRISCILLA: But what happened to us as a family was that we welcomed her questioning mind as long as she was questioning the same things we were questioning. When all of a sudden she would come out with an opinion that seemed to us wild, or questioned something that to us seemed unquestionable, we would become very defensive.

Bob: For instance, like when she asked, "Why do you stand up when they raise the flag?"

Priscilla: There's much less that we back away from now. I'm not afraid now of just saying, "I don't know why I feel such and such is true, but I do." I don't feel that I have to apologize for having opinions, just as a person, that perhaps I can't back up with facts.

So the Bernards' daughter is highly emotional, dependent on others, has a great need for attention and a great need for group approval. She also has a flair for the dramatic, which was demonstrated very early with her tantrums and nosebleeds. She has a high intellect and finds satisfaction in using it to question established standards. But there seems to be nothing in all this that would inherently doom her early teen years to the runaway and drug pattern. The description essentially fits ten thousand other kids who play it straight. It just happens that Ellie made some decisions that were different from those the straight kids make. Even she probably does not know all of the "why."

Bob and Priscilla are willing to accept whatever blame may be justly theirs.

Priscilla: Having a stable home doesn't necessarily mean that you are not going to influence your child in a way that you don't anticipate. For instance, I think in recommending books to her that I had read I was probably pushing her in what you might call a liberal direction, at an age when emotionally she couldn't handle it. And also, since her contemporaries in school were not necessarily worried about the problems of society—they were more interested in when they would be able to wear their first bras, or when the first boy would ask them for a date—I think it may have intensified her desire to be with older kids. There was another thing too. At a very early age, Ellie had adult acceptance. We would have friends in and they would include her as an adult in the conversation. And I think because she wanted to be aware of the world situation and wanted to be a thinking individual, we encouraged this.

Bob: Quite frequently we included Ellie in the discussion of problems that involved family decision-making.

Priscilla: I still don't know if that was wrong.

Bob: It might have been wrong for Ellie, but it might be right for the boys. [Jeff is ten and Edward eight.] We don't really plan to do a lot of things differently with the boys than what we've done with Ellie. We don't know how they're going to react, but we've got to take the chance. As parents we have to help them develop.

Priscilla: We have to help them become adults. If they get the idea that contributing to the making of family decisions entitles them to be completely independent from the family—well, it's sort of a wild chance you have to take.

Bob: Someday they're going to have to make decisions, and you don't just learn to make decisions in a vacuum. You have to have some experience. What better place to get experience than through the family group?

Was this, then, the Bernards' critical mistake—that they tried to encourage an inquiring mind? Perhaps. But if so, it is a pattern of tragedy in a classic tradition:

literature is filled with characters who bring suffering upon themselves because of a virtue held to excess.

Most parents of runaway kids will finecomb their memories to come up with "reasons." Most will latch on to one past incident or another to define where they "went wrong." But this is a very simplistic and most likely false solution to the question of why the child wandered. The question Why? is so complex that there may literally be no definable answer to it. Pinpointing the blame and flagellating oneself can only drain energy —energy that could be better used for building a framework for forgiveness: forgiveness of one's youngster, and forgiveness of oneself.

2

"A SWINGER KIND
OF KID"

DEPENDING UPON how she wears her long hair, Ellie looks like Alice in Wonderland or one of the Alice's Restaurant crowd. The "sweet young thing" look is as genuine as the hippie look. She has very large brown eyes, high cheekbones, and that phenomenal attribute for a teenager, a flawlessly smooth complexion. She is a pleasure to look at.

Now seventeen, she does not see herself as a pleasure to look at. And apparently it has not always been true.

ELLIE: When I was a kid I was really ugly. I mean really grotesquely ugly: buck teeth, and braids, and glasses. And people used to put me down because of it. They'd call me Ugly, and call me Buck Teeth Beaver, and all that stuff. So I had these feelings of rejection. Even when I finally started looking better, I just still had these pent-up feelings.

PRISCILLA: Ellie had a severe orthodontial problem. You wouldn't know it to look at her now. She became very self-conscious about meeting new people. Fortunately, we were able to have the corrective work done earlier than can be done with most children, so she was out of the braces by the time she'd finished sixth grade. But I think all this contributed to her need for approval. I think even now she has feelings of insecurity.

BOB: She's always appeared outwardly very self-confident and cocky.

PRISCILLA: And really she's so squishy underneath.

BOB: Yes. Even as parents, it has taken us an awful long time to really understand the defense mechanism. I remember when she was just beginning to get into trouble I went in and sat on the side of her bed, and she burst into tears and said what an ugly person she was, and how bad she was. She was very self-condemnatory.

PRISCILLA: She sets tremendously high standards for herself and she's very quick to feel a complete sense of failure if she doesn't meet those standards.

All that notwithstanding, Ellie came out of elementary school riding the top of the wave. She had received all A's. She was the valedictorian of her eighth-grade class. She was invited to play a Gershwin tune on the piano at the graduation ceremony, and to accompany the violinist.

She had also received a mild kind of fame—or noto-

riety—through her first protest song, written for a talent
assembly at the grade school. Now she remembers only
snatches of it. It went something like this:

Where can I hide? Where can I run?
I'm always accompanied by the bullets' hum.
Bombs are bursting everywhere, on the land and in
    the air.
Drop that H-bomb, drop it quick—
Don't think while you drop it, for you may get sick,
Don't think of the people that must die,
Don't think of your friends for you may cry.
The world is filled with words of hate.
Do it now or it'll be too late—
Kill that Negro, kill that Jew,
Kill your friend or he'll kill you!

Parents of the schoolchildren did not hear Ellie sing
her song. What they did hear was the interpretation
brought home by youngsters too unsophisticated to understand the subtleties of satire. Ellie's former principal
good-naturedly recalls, "We almost had the whole Anti-
Defamation League on our necks for that one!"

Ellie was apparently unaffected, or at least unabashed,
by the controversy.

ELLIE: I had just learned to play the guitar, and I was
really into the thing where good ol' Ellie was gonna become a famous rock singer. At that time a bunch of
protest songs were coming out. Bob Dylan was at his
height. And I decided I was gonna write a song. It just
kind of came to me. And I guess it was a pretty good
song for an eighth-grader. That's all I could say for it
now, that it was a pretty good song for an eighth-grader.

My parents were really enthused about it, y'know? I guess it had a kind of sentimental value, because it was my first. But the melody is uninventive. It's just a blah melody, and the words are contrived.

Whatever she thinks of it now, it appears to have at least represented to her then a step toward participation in the protest fad of older teens.

"Ellie was always a swinger kind of kid," her elementary principal says.

ELLIE: I was really fascinated with—well, in those days it was the beatniks, 'cause the hippies hadn't come out yet. I was really digging the beatnik thing. I wanted to go to Greenwich Village and be a beatnik, even when I was just in seventh grade.

QUESTION: Did you and your friends talk about this sort of thing?

ELLIE: No, none of my friends was cool. Like I always had to watch what I'd say in front of my friends, because they were the type that—well, for instance, they are now the "soshes" [social climbers] in high school. So I never had anybody to rap with [talk confidentially to].

Q: Did you know anyone in elementary school that was on drugs?

ELLIE: Yeah, I knew one guy. He was a couple of years older and he was one of my close friends. He was taking dope, but I didn't really feel like doing it then. I wanted to find out some more about it.

So Ellie was feeling the "call of the wild" as early as seventh grade. But there were no major incidents in elementary school.

ELLIE: I think I started on the wrong road the summer between elementary school and high school. We moved from southern California up north. But that summer we stayed with my grandmother, who lives about seventy-five miles from where we moved. I started hanging around with people six years older than me. I had a boyfriend that summer. He was a freshman in college and I was just going into high school. These older friends were hipster-type people. They were using drugs, but I still didn't take any yet. But I thought, If they're doing it, that's cool, because I dig these people and it must be the thing to do.

PRISCILLA: My young brother Tom is part of the older crowd Ellie got into. It was his best friend that Ellie dated that summer. My brother is a particular favorite of Ellie's, and so is his girl friend [now his wife]. Ellie was accepted by their whole crowd. I found out since, however, that much of the acceptance was sympathy. She would magnify stories of the hard life she had at home and make herself a really dramatic figure. They were feeling terribly sorry for her.

BOB: I was depicted as being an ogre: she "had to" take her meals in her own bedroom and "couldn't" sit at the table with us.

PRISCILLA: My brother knew this wasn't so, but I think he thought it was kind of funny just to let her go on. But the other kids didn't necessarily know it wasn't so. Then we moved on to our new home in a nearby community. Ellie had liked being with my brother's older group, so in our new situation she immediately sought out girls that were of college age. Well, of course the restrictions that we had to put on Ellie at age fourteen were much different from those the eighteen-year-olds had: they were driving, they had much later curfew, they were dating often, and so forth. So anytime that we would say, "No, you can't," just confirmed her picture of herself as being very abused and very unloved, because we weren't allowing her to do the things that all her friends were doing. That's part of why she started using marijuana. At that point in Ellie's development, she hardly would have been able to turn it down. She had to prove that she was as old emotionally as these other kids.

ELLIE: I got into this folk-singing group and the youngest chick in it except for me was a senior in high school. The other two were in college. One of the college girls turned me on to my first dope. I was spending the night at her house. I smoked a whole joint of Acapulco Gold, which is some of the strongest grass you can get. That kind of did me in right there. I was pretty stoned. Then this chick who gave it to me shared another one with me, so I had like one and a half. I was pretty out of it. I just laid down on her bed and closed my eyes.

The Bernards, of course, had no awareness of Ellie's first "trip," nor of those that followed.

BOB: For one thing, she had quite honestly told us about the other girl being on marijuana, but she had said, "I don't need that stuff." And we believed her.

PRISCILLA: For some reason we had no suspicion. I guess we would have expected more outward signs. Or we thought that we would have just sort of known. She has since told us that she was very careful about never using marijuana in the house or where we would see evidence of it.

Undoubtedly any parent today would be much quicker to suspect trouble. The huge bulk of publicity about teens on drugs has appeared since Ellie first began her drug experience. At this stage, for the Bernards, the idea of Ellie's "turning on" at age fourteen was so remote that there appeared to be no reason to even consider it.

Unfortunately many parents even now find it hard to accept their child's involvement with drugs. Even though every medium of mass communication now pelts us with information to the contrary, many parents still cling to the hope that only the "bad" kids go the drug route, or kids whose parents don't care what they do. On both counts, the case of the Bernard family (among thousands of others) shoots that theory down.

You, THE READER: Our family is regarded as stalwart in the community. Our children are bright and accomplished and well-mannered. They have never been a source of real trouble. There has never been evidence of drugs around our home.

Us: Great. Maybe all *is* well. But don't automatically bank on that. The *fact* is, if your youngster is enrolled in a public school, if he goes to drive-in theaters or restaurants, if he attends football games or goes to parties, yes, even if he goes to a youth fellowship at church—if he has, in short, been out of your sight at all over the past few months, then it is STRONGLY likely that he has been invited, or even challenged, *over and over again,* to smoke, swallow, and inject drugs of one kind or another. Drugs in all forms are indeed that available.

And not from evil little men lurking on street corners, but from kids that look, act, talk, and *are* just like your youngsters. Nor are drugs available only to older teens. Whereas Ellie knew only one "doper" in elementary school five years ago, now in many elementary schools she would be surrounded by them.

Most of us normal, decent parents like to think that our children will be equipped to say no when confronted with the lure of drugs. But we must remember that they hear us saying yes to that lure all the time: alcohol is a drug. (Did you know that?) So are sleeping pills, obviously. And tranquilizers. And diet pills. And pep pills. And so on into the night. The difference between the drugs we take and the drugs our kids take is simply that we usually can obtain our drugs legally. There is no difference in the effect on our mental and physiological systems. Some of our drugs are just as distorting as theirs. Often the difference is not even in the amount used, for we too tend to use drugs to excess. And our *excessive* use of legal drugs is no more moral than the illegal use of drugs by our youngsters. If excessive use is immoral, it *is* immoral—whether or not it is legal! And our kids know this, so we must face it too.

If our youngsters can trust us to be consistent and fair, they will not be afraid that we will condemn them while whitewashing ourselves. We have no right, no right whatever, to expect more from them in terms of morality than we expect from ourselves. Our kids feel this very, very keenly.

YOU (PERHAPS): All right, I understand. So I should be worthy of my youngsters' trust. But you are pretty casual about suggesting that maybe *they* are not to be trusted, after all.

Us (FOR SURE): We didn't mean to suggest that! Of course you should trust them! But realistically, not sentimentally! Trust that your child is basically moral, but don't trust him not to be tempted. Trust him to believe in basically the same values we do (h'mmm, is that always good?) but don't trust him not to occasionally place peer-group values above ours. Trust your child to want to be "good," but don't trust him not to test what is or isn't good. In other words, *it isn't fair to your child to trust him in a sentimental way*, because that doesn't allow him to become his own person.

Sentimental trust is, in a sense, really a club hanging over your child's head. It is inscribed, "I trust you to be perfect, and you had better live up to that trust, or else!" When such "trust" is broken, as it will inevitably be, very often the relationship between parent and teen is broken too. Hurt piles on hurt for both. The youngster feels less and less self-worth in the face of deeper and deeper parental disappointment and disapproval. And the parent feels more and more guilty and rejected in the face of greater and greater efforts by the youngster to assert his independence and, thereby, his own sense of worth.

Realistic trust, on the other hand, is more like a bridge. It is inscribed: "I have faith in you. If you should fall into a mire, I trust you not to want to wallow in it for long, but to want to find a way out." The bridge supports the youngster's sense of self-worth. And it is just that—a bridge that is *there* when the youngster is ready to use it.

Realistic trust has some grace for parents too. The parent who trusts in his child's basic goodness—strongly, but not sentimentally—is not devastated when the child yields to temptation along the way to adulthood. The props of his child's perfection are not knocked out from under the parent. He does not have to defend his own vulnerability as the parent of a child "gone bad." He has no need to shield himself with bitterness. He may be hurt, he may even be angry, but he has more compassion for his youngster than sorrow for himself.

Just as sentimental trust produces a cycle of hurt, so realistic trust can produce a more hopeful cycle. The parent trusts in his child's *basic* integrity. *And the child can trust him to do so!* The teen can trust that his parents approve of *him,* though perhaps not of his decisions or actions. That leaves him a lot of room to do his growing in.

If realistic trust frees the child to become his own person, it also frees the parent to declare himself, to set down some rules. Teens need to know their limits. They will buck them, they will try to go beyond them, they will profess to hate them, but they *need* the security of knowing where their limits are. One of the problems with sentimental trust is that it tends to wonder if rules belie the trust. The parents say, "We're going to stay up to be sure you are in by twelve o'clock." The youngster cries, "You don't trust me!" And the parents are stumped for an answer. But the truth is, the kid keeps coming in at *two* o'clock. He really *can't* be trusted in this instance! But he has this amazing ability to make his parents feel guilty by *accusing them:* "You don't trust me!" The club is turned on the parents.

This "You don't trust me" plea is a huge problem for sentimental trust. Some parents, in order to dodge the club, choose to adopt a laissez-faire policy toward their

teens' behavior—no guidelines are laid, precisely so that
the kids will feel that they are trusted! Such sentimen-
tality backfires. Kids are apt to go farther and farther,
seeking the security of limits.

It backfires another way too. One young teen, whose
very loving parents set down no rules, looked around
one day and noticed that other girls had to be in by
eleven, other girls couldn't go to certain night spots,
other girls couldn't date more than twice a week. And
she seriously, sadly, raised the question, "Sometimes I
wonder if my parents love me."

The "You don't trust me" syndrome is less of a problem for realistic trust. Realistic trust can say, in effect:
"Well, I *don't* trust you *in this particular situation*. And
I'll keep on setting the limits, so you'll know where I
stand." The parent is not blackmailed into keeping hands
off by the accusation, "You don't trust me." The youngster
is not cut down by an attack on his *basic* integrity; but
he is still brought face to face with his own ability to
make an error: "I have a great deal of faith in you as a
person, but you've given me no evidence that you can
be trusted in this particular situation at this particular
time." The erring youngster knows his parents will not
wink away his transgression, but he also knows that their
relationship, though perhaps bent a little, is not altogether
broken.

3
THE BIG FAVOR

OF HER FIRST EXPERIENCE ON POT, Ellie says: "I don't think it was either a pleasant experience or an unpleasant one. It was just kind of there, and I was going through it."

However, the experience appears to have "locked her in" to her new circle of older friends. She was no longer an outsider in terms of their drug experience. Her older friends had done her "the big favor." They had turned her on.

This spirit of evangelism is common to many teen-age dopers. There seems to be a need to do others the "favor" of introducing them to the world of drugs. Delbert L. Earisman, in his excellent little book *Hippies in Our*

Midst (Fortress Press, 1968), tells of a girl who wishes she could return to the church of her upbringing, Jehovah's Witnesses, and put LSD into the punch, because "they are all such beautiful people and deserve to be turned on." Some teens talk with glee of their fantasy of turning their parents on. Ellie too chuckles a bit as she recalls how, on one of the many runaway excursions she was to take, she and some others "turned on" the elderly relatives of a friend. "We turned his mother on to acid, and we turned his uncle on to acid, and all these elderly people were just really tripping out."

For some, the evangelism may be honestly a matter of wanting to include their friends in on what they regard as a fascinating experience. For others, wanting to share the experience of drugs has a purely economic base. To be a dealer in drugs is an easy way to make a lot of money, and is easier yet if you have your own clientele.

On the other hand, some kids have convinced themselves that the drug experience helps them to relate to others better, to communicate better. This may be part of the interest some have in turning their parents on. In spite of the break they have deliberately made from their families, many youngsters admit movingly, "I know I love my parents." Some fantasize that if they and their parents could take a "trip" together they would have a whole new and wonderful set of relationships. However, teens, like the rest of us, are contradictory souls, and most would regard a turned-on mom or pop as an intrusion into private territory.

The "better communication" bit is a favorite excuse among teen-agers for turning others on to drugs. But there is another consideration, one that not many of the kids could recognize, or admit if they did recognize it. It lies in a certain amused and patronizing attitude that always seems to come through when a youngster talks about doing anyone, parents or peers, the big favor. This attitude has something to do with a feeling of power. There is the exhilaration of having power over someone else, of causing someone else to join one's rebellious ranks, of laughing (perhaps gently, but laughing nonetheless) at someone who is walking for the first time down a road one has himself traveled many times. There is camaraderie in the laughter, but there is an edge of superiority too: the evangelist has made another convert.

The question is, Why was it so easy? We've already recognized that we cannot presume to come up with a formula of the reasons any one youngster from any one family goes the drug route. Still there are some general factors that help explain, in an external sort of way, why a youngster with a "good" upbringing and good advantages can be such an easy mark for his friends.

Probably experimenting with drugs has little to do with parental hassling, though that's a common peg for youngsters to hang it on. Some counseling groups are discovering, however, that the real adolescent-parent tension comes *after* the youngster is on the drugs. (That should take some of the pressure off anxious parents!)

What then? The peer group? The war for independence? Both of these are, of course, formidable pressures and both are involved with the adolescent's identity crisis. If his friends are on drugs, the adolescent confirms his security within the group by taking them too. And if his parents object, as of course they must if they

care, then taking drugs confirms his independence from
their current ability to influence his life.

There is nothing new we can offer in this book on the
topics of the peer group and the drive for independence.
A thousand other books have said it all earlier and
better, so we will not elaborate here. But the strength
of these two pressures cannot be minimized. And, as
parents consider what's happening to their child, neither
of these two factors should seem unnatural to them, at
least not at their core. All of us have been there too, on
that frantic escalator to maturity that is called the teens.
We may have handled it better, but the need for peer-
group acceptance and the drive for independence were
the oil for our escalators too. This is not to say, of course,
that to understand these pressures is to condone them as
excuses. The problem is ever, How much oil is enough,
and when does it begin to damage the machinery?

There are two other considerations as to why kids can
be quick converts to dope. But they are such simple
ideas, and so basic, that they are often overlooked, or
disbelieved as being too easy.

One is plain, old, ordinary curiosity! Printed and elec-
tronic words daily describe the wonders of marijuana,
of the psychedelics, and even of glue-sniffing, in great,
enticing, juicy detail. For society to castigate the youngster for being curious is like waving the carrot in front
of the donkey, then kicking him for going for it. Who
could expect an alert youngster to hear of a scintillating
LSD trip and not be tempted to experience it for himself? For that matter, who can deny his *own* curiosity
about it all?

Sometimes curiosity coalesces into the drive for independence. If curiosity is stronger than the parental no-no, behold, a ready-made situation for asserting oneself!

Parents need to be sensitive to the curiosity factor. In spite of its reputation for contributing to the demise of cats, curiosity is normally a very healthy and creative phenomenon. The problem is, of course, that in the case of drugs it seems almost inseparable from temptation. And again, though we obviously do not condone the yielding to curiosity-temptation, we do have to recognize its quickened reality for teen-agers.

There is yet another very simple factor in why some kids are attracted to drugs: some teens maintain that they like the sensation drugs give them. The fact that they say they feel that way makes us concerned and worried adults even more concerned and worried. But still we have to start where the youngsters say they are, not just where we feel they ought to be.

We know there are bad trips. We know there are overdoses that kill. We know there are those whose minds will not ever return to normal. We know there is at least speculation about damage to unborn generations. We know the whole drug scene has potential for dissipation, and waste, and even horror. And our kids have heard it all too. But the only thing that has any sense of reality for them is their own experience. Their experience tells them that drugs give them a "different" kind of sensation. Everything else—all the frantic warnings and all the worried pleas—all of it is remote and unreal and "It-won't-happen-to-me-because-I-can-handle-it."

So we have to start "where it's at": our youngsters are curious, and, at least until a bad trip hits them, they think that drugs have something to offer them.

If we fail to understand the pull of curiosity and pleasure, if we regard it as not sophisticated enough, or complicated enough, or significant enough to "get to" *our* youngster, then the youngster will feel he has to defend his actions by latching on to other, more "important" reasons. Reasons such as "I can't stand school," or "The world is going to hell" may have an element of truth to them, but they are probably not the ultimate motivating factor in the child's decision to go on drugs. They are cushioning excuses, but they do nothing to help the youngster assume his own responsibility for his decision.

Therefore, it will not be helpful for us to approach the drug problem with our own defenses up and our judge's robes on. Being able to understand and, more than that, to *identify* with the factors of curiosity and pleasure will at least *help* to keep the channels of communication open between parent and child.

The youngster needs to know that we don't approve of his own personal drug scene. *But he also needs to know that we understand something of what's happened to him.* That way, we're resisting his *attraction to drugs,* not just hassling *him.*

4
"NO FAVOR AT ALL, MAN!"

ELLIE WAS JUST BARELY FOURTEEN when she smoked that first marijuana cigarette. Not long afterward, she made her first, tentative flight from home.

ELLIE: I forget why I ran away the first time. My parents were hassling me, but I can't even remember what for. I had long hair, though, I remember that. I went to school in the morning and went into the washroom at the break, and cut my hair off short. Then I took a bus to the town where my boyfriend was, the boy I had met that summer.

Q: Was the haircut an attempt to disguise yourself?

ELLIE: Yeah. It was an ugly attempt. My hair looked so funky.

The Bernards felt differently about it.

BOB: When we saw her haircut, we thought it looked very nice.

PRISCILLA: I guess we thought it was an improvement because it made her look more like a schoolgirl freshman.

Ellie never really had a chance to see if the disguise would have worked. Bob and Priscilla had a pretty good idea of where she had gone. With the help of Priscilla's brother, they had her at her grandmother's house within a few hours. She spent the night there, and the next morning returned home for a tearful reunion.

PRISCILLA: She was very happy to be home. I think she had a bit of a shock in finding that her poor boyfriend was just about frightened out of his mind when she showed up there. He had dated her a few times, and he liked her, but it was certainly nothing of a serious nature. And of course his first thought was, "My gosh, she's fourteen years old, and she's on my doorstep!"

Ellie laughs about it now. "I was so stupid! I didn't even know I could have gotten the boy in trouble just by being there."

The Bernards moved back to southern California the second semester of that freshman year, and Ellie was enrolled in high school with her former grade school friends.

ELLIE: Boy! Was that a mess! All the kids I knew before were now "soshes," and though I was not really a doper, I took dope. I didn't want anything to do with the "soshes." But I didn't have any friends. Like, everybody in that school just ignores you.

So toward the end of school there's this cat that sits next to me in algebra. I hadn't even smoked any grass lately, 'cause I didn't know any good connections. But he and I used to talk about it. So one day he pulls some pills out of his pocket. I said, "What's that?" And he says, "They're whites." I didn't even know what whites were. And he goes, "You mean you haven't had any of these?" And I go, "No." So he gave me two whites. They're the stimulants, the uppers, y'know? From there we had to go to an assembly. The effects started coming on, and I felt just like running around the whole auditorium. After the assembly he gave me another one, so I was speeding pretty fast.

By the time I got home I was still going, but I knew enough not to blow it in front of my parents, y'know? So I just forced myself to remain fairly quiet.

After that, after I took those whites, all of a sudden I just started meeting all the dopers in school.

Recently, in an informal conversation with a group of teens, Ellie remarked quite passionately: "That boy that turned me on to my first whites did me no favor! No favor at all, man!"

BOB: I think our first awareness that Ellie was using drugs of any kind was one evening she came in and turned on the phonograph, and pulled the drapes, and started dancing—

PRISCILLA: —which she does from time to time anyway. Sometimes she does it as an exercise, but this went on and on and on.

BOB: Bedtime came and she went to her room. But she stayed awake reading. I got up to check on her once, but then I went back to bed and fell asleep myself. When I woke up again, she was in the front room, dancing again. I got her to go back to bed, but she kept her light on so she could read.

PRISCILLA: Twice after that I woke up and went into her room. She kept saying, "I'm just not tired!"

BOB: It was a week or more before we realized—

PRISCILLA: We kept puzzling over what sort of physical changes she was going through because of adolescence that could have caused her behavior. And of course now I'm sure it would hit any parent faster because there is so much more publicity about drugs. We tightened up our rules again then, saying we didn't want her to see this or that person.

BOB: But other problems began to show up then too. She had always been used to being an outstanding student. But she was very far from that now.

ELLIE: My grades were slipping and I didn't really give a damn.

PRISCILLA: And then she very much resented the ruling that freshmen aren't allowed to take certain classes, or to take much of a part in the life of the school. So she looked for a group that would accept her, and would allow her to take part in various activities, even though they were not school-sanctioned. We learned later about her interest in S.D.S. activities, for instance.

As her sophomore year began, Ellie's problems began to intensify. In September she ran away for what amounted to three days. (She returned for a few hours during that time.) None of the family clearly remembers why she left, other than it was something related to the whole general problem.

Priscilla: I think it was something she had been called into the school office for.

Ellie: The reasons I ran away were really trivial, just about always.

Priscilla: Whatever the problem was, we talked it out somewhat before Bob had to leave for a rare business trip. He was scheduled to stop over in Illinois to visit his parents first.

Bob: My parting words to Ellie were, "Don't do anything to spoil my trip. I'll be back next Thursday and we can get this thing all straightened out." I got to Illinois and was there with my parents only about four hours when I got a call from Priscilla saying that Ellie had run away.

Priscilla: We discussed what action I should take and I reported to the authorities that she was missing. Two or three hours later I received a call from the Diggers Society [a group of hippies loosely banded together for mutual support]. They reported that Ellie was under their wing out on Sunset Strip in Hollywood, and I should come and get her. [The Bernards' difficult experience with the Diggers is described in Chapter 8.]

Bob: When they got Ellie back home, they called me again. I told her to stay home and to stay calm. That was Friday night. The next morning I got another call from Priscilla, saying, "She's gone again." So I had no alternative but to take a plane and get on back. We found her Monday afternoon, over in the Hollywood area. A young friend where I work, a hippie type, knew all the hangouts, so he went out to find her for us. He talked her into coming back voluntarily. She came home with a boy she wanted to marry. She had met him Saturday, and wanted to marry him Monday.

PRISCILLA: She wasn't quite fifteen. She was about two days away from her fifteenth birthday.

BOB: The boy was actually psychopathic. It was really terrible. He kept volunteering the information that he had never been in any trouble with the law. But when we told Ellie that the only way that they could be married would be by approval of a judge, he nearly panicked. "Oh, I don't want to go anywhere near a court! I don't want to go anywhere near 'the man,'" he said. He almost went out through the window!

ELLIE: This boy and I had gone through a hippie marriage ceremony on Sunset Strip. The cat was really a scrounge. He was a pathological liar. He was really, really a cruddy guy, y'know? My parents said they would not let us get legally married. Thank God for that! [Laughter in voice.] Oh, if I were stuck with that creep now—oh, boy!

Ellie came home, got back into high school, and then started going with the real dope crowd.

ELLIE: Like, before I was just kind of on the outskirts of it. But now I was a real doper, y'know? At school they had a list of kids that were suspected dealers. And I and all my friends were in the top ten of the list of two hundred. One day the school called my parents and said, "Your daughter is a Communist and a drug dealer."

Q: A Communist?

ELLIE: Yes, because I was distributing leaflets for S.D.S., and trying to start an underground newspaper, and raising questions about the flag. My parents hadn't been aware of my interest in S.D.S. or in the underground paper, or anything. I was pretty sneaky. Like, they also weren't aware I was dealing. When I came home that day, my parents searched my purse. There were a couple of notes in there from different kids, saying, "Can you score a lid for me, Ellie?"

Q: Translated, that means—

ELLIE: "Can you get me some grass?" I also had a bunch of paraphernalia for S.D.S. in my purse—and just about everything my parents didn't want to find. So they decided it was all because of the group I was in, y'know? So they wanted the names of all my friends. I refused to tell them because I thought my friends would all get busted. My parents were pretty upset with me. And so the next morning, the day before Thanksgiving, I ran away. I went to Fresno.

Q: How did you know where to go?

ELLIE: One of my close friends was like *the* dealer at school. I sneaked a call to her that night and told her the situation. She had a friend in Fresno, so she phoned her and told her to expect me.

PRISCILLA: Ellie had drawn such a dramatic picture of how strict we as parents were, that she got herself into a trap. Her friends believed her stories, and began encouraging her to run away: "I wouldn't take that—I'd split!" She has since said that all of a sudden she felt she was in such a position that she *had* to run away: if these unreasonable things really had happened, her friends would think less and less of her if she should stay and endure them.

Early on that morning before Thanksgiving, when Bob went out to the car to go to work, there was Ellie standing in the backyard. He asked her what she was doing. "Oh, I'm just gathering leaves for my biology class."

Fine. Could he help her?

"Oh, Daddy, would you?"

So he helped her gather leaves, then she went back inside and he went on to work.

When Ellie left for school, Priscilla watched her go to make sure she headed off in the right direction. "I guess I had a feeling she would run off that day."

What she did was circle around the block and come back into her own yard to pick up the guitar and duffel bag she had thrown out of her bedroom window. Obviously, she had been trying to leave earlier when Bob had spotted her in the yard.

As the morning progressed, Priscilla began to see signs of Ellie's leaving. Particularly, her expensive guitar was standing where her old one usually did. Her dad had told Ellie, "If you ever run off again, don't take your good guitar with you." So she didn't. She took the old one and placed the good one where her mother might think the old one was in its normal place. Later, at another time when she ran off again, she took the good guitar with her and did indeed have it stolen from her within a few days.

Asked if she hoped that running away would make her

parents feel sorry for her because she would be all alone and out in the world on a holiday, she replied: "Not really. I just hoped they were hurtin'. I felt like I wanted to ruin their Thanksgiving."

Looking back on it, the Bernards remember one moment of comic relief to make them smile a bit through their tears. On Thanksgiving Day, their two little boys came to them and said they had been thinking about the chores Ellie had to do, and that they would be taking over the chores now. Edward was going to take out the trash, and Jeff was going to set the table, one of them would bring in the newspaper, and so forth.

PRISCILLA: We thought this was wonderfully thoughtful.

BOB: Then Jeff said, "And we're going to split Ellie's allowance!"

Ellie wanted to ruin Thanksgiving for her parents, and it was within her power to do so. The natural result of her running off would be, of course, a couple of "hurtin'" parents. But there is another kind of power that parents of kids on drugs often *hand* to their youngsters, a power that is *not* natural for them to have. It is innocently given, but it brings unnatural results. A father says, for instance, "I'd do anything—sell my house, my business, anything—to get my boy off drugs." Zap! The central power of the household has just been transferred to the youngster!

It happens, again, when parents are afraid to say no to their drug-addicted children, lest it drive them to further rebellion. The addiction becomes a very effective lever for the youngster in getting the household run the way he wants it run. One father speaks of how shocked his son was when he finally told the boy he could not have the family car because he is not a responsible person while on drugs. "It was the first time in months I hadn't catered to him!"

Transfer of power also happens when a parent favors the one youngster over others because, "Remember, he's on drugs." (That doesn't do much for sibling relationships, either!)

Sometimes parents even try to make changes in the pattern of their own lives, hoping that new behavior will please their youngster enough to get him off drugs. "He doesn't like my friends, so I don't have them over much anymore."

None of this is effective, because all of it is wheedling. None of it helps the youngster face the responsibility of his own actions—except that he probably notices that his actions have resulted in greater power within the family! The role of the *parent* is to be the center of control in the family. Youngsters are not entitled to, and should not be burdened by, this kind of near-absolute power. When parents allow their kids to usurp power, rather than to have a share in it, the family situation is in deep trouble, whether or not the youngster is a doper, and whether he runs or stays.

In another vein, it is interesting that in the case of the Bernards, neither Ellie nor her parents can clearly remember the specific reasons for her leaving those first two times. This could be just some sort of block, of course. But at least it says that none of them is clinging to all the things that hurt. They will not bring them out as ammunition in future times of tension. This is illustrative of a hugely potent concept: "Love keeps no score of wrongs." (This is the New English Bible translation of I Cor. 13:6.)

Be we parent or teen, this concept takes our injured pride, and our need to justify our own actions, and our need to have the last word, and makes them all completely invalid. We toss away that which nourishes these needs when we toss away that list of the other's faults.

Love keeps no score of wrongs! (It may be easier for us to give up score-keeping on one another if we remind ourselves that Another gave up score-keeping on us long ago.)

Love keeps no score of wrongs, not even between a parent and his drug-attracted teen-ager!

When the truth of this verse shapes our relationship to each other, then the next verse, "There is nothing love cannot face," offers us hope, and rationale—and a head start!—for genuine reconciliation.

5

INTO CUSTODY

ELLIE WAS GONE SIX WEEKS on that third runaway trip—
past Christmas and into the new year. She had her first
LSD experience in Fresno. Later she hitchhiked to Santa
Barbara with a girl friend, and spent Christmas with a
"family of hip people," the parents of which were apparently not hip enough to recognize Ellie as a runaway.
Then she and a boy, also apparently a wanderer, took a
train to San Francisco. In the Haight-Ashbury district
they met some people who were going to Seattle that
night.

ELLIE: So we went up to Seattle and stayed with these
people up there. When we came back to Frisco we

stayed in their pad in the Haight-Ashbury. Something happened to the guy that I went up there with. He was a horse player. I don't know, I think he got lost on a horse track or something. Anyway, he never came back!

When I got to Frisco—oh, boy!—was I dropping acid, like every day. I was dealing then too, pushing acid and grass and cocaine and whatever else we had around. This pad I was living in had like four of the biggest dealers in San Francisco. And so I dealt.

Then four of us went up to Sacramento for a few days. When I got back to the pad the first thing I heard was, "Ellie, there's a message for you at Huckleberry House." Huckleberry House is a sort of contact place for runaways. The message was from my father. It said to call him. When I did, he goes, "Ellie, can you come home tonight?" I didn't want to come home. I just wasn't ready to come home. But I could tell my parents were crying, so I really felt pressured. Finally I said, "No, I can't come home tonight." And he goes, "How come?" and I go, "Because I'm going to drop some acid."

Finally Ellie agreed to return home the following day, and arrangements were made for her uncle's girl friend to pick her up and get her to the San Francisco airport. But in the meantime, Ellie "dropped a bunch of acid."

ELLIE: When I got on the airplane the passenger-relations man knew something was wrong with me. I hadn't slept in about three weeks because of all the dope I was taking. My eyes were just wasted, just pure dilated. And I looked like a freak. I had on this old long shirt, and a pair of really ripped-up blue jeans, and a bunch of beads and stuff, y'know? And I was really a stoned mess. They got me on the plane, but the passenger-relations man asked, "Who is hip? What's wrong with her?" a girl goes, "She just dropped some acid. She'll be O.K." And the guy starts blabbering something about altitude not mixing with acid. So they came and yanked me off the plane. They yanked me off the plane and wouldn't tell me why, y'know? It was really traumatic because I was really tripping heavy. We called my parents, and I spent the night with my grandmother, and flew home the next day.

Ellie was home a day or two and then was placed in juvenile hall. She remained there for about a week but spent the whole time in the infirmary. Too many pills, too much exposure to the winter weather, and improper diet had laid her low.

When she was released from juvenile hall, she was made a ward of the court. That was on a Friday. On Sunday night she ran away again.

Ellie says she ran this time because she was "really uptight" at having been locked up, and because her parents had placed restrictions on which friends she would be allowed to see. In addition, her parents feel there was an element of apprehension. "She hadn't seen the probation officer yet, and didn't know what the officer would say, nor what kind of legal rules would be set down." At that point in her life, it seemed easier to split than to face the problem.

She really didn't get very far this time. She was picked up the next evening by the highway patrol, hitchhiking on a nearby freeway. (This turned out to be the only one of her five runaway experiences from which she did not return home of her own volition.) This time, as a ward of the court, she was put directly into juvenile hall.

PRISCILLA: Supposedly juvenile hall is a sort of way-station. Youngsters are put there and expected to stay there for one to four weeks, hopefully not longer than that, until placement is made for them. Unfortunately, in most cases it doesn't work out that way. In most cases there are no places to put them. The authorities won't let them come home, and justifiably. I'm sure if she had come home, she wouldn't have stayed home. So she was in juvenile hall for four months. And what she was when she came out of there was very different from when she went in. At least, when she went in, she had a cause: it was her life and she was going to live it her way. She was rebellious, but she had a cause to rebel about. When she came out she was very bitter and very surly. Her language was dreadful. Her whole outlook was terrible.

BOB: She's been down there about fourteen weeks, and the maximum they told us they'd keep her there was four weeks. They kept extending it and extending it. We could just see the complete deterioration. And in addition to her whole bitter attitude toward life, and the language degeneration, she was gaining excessive weight. Every week, when we'd visit Ellie, all the girls there looked heavier and heavier.

Ellie had "had it" with the place too. At one point, she took the matter of getting out into her own hands.

PRISCILLA: We received a really wild letter from her, describing suicidal tendencies and declaring she was manic-depressive.

Q: Did she use that terminology?

PRISCILLA: Yes, exact terminology. Meantime, our minister friend went down to visit Ellie and Ellie pulled the same thing on him. There were tears and laughter and tears again, and "I can't stand this place anymore," and "Get me out of here."

BOB: We contacted the probation officer, and she laughed. She pointed out that if Ellie had actually been in the condition she described, she would not have been able to describe it so clinically well. Also, Ellie went right from the description of her condition into something very nice that had happened.

PRISCILLA: Oh, yes: the letter went from all about that manic-depressive thing to how there'd been an assembly and she'd won some sort of prize. So we all decided to just sort of hang loose until the next Sunday, when Bob and I could see her again. When we finally did, she started pleading, "You don't care for me, or you wouldn't want to see me going crazy and not try to help me." So we explained that she would have to talk to the people there at juvenile hall, and they'd have to take it to a judge, and he might commit her if it were really of that serious a nature. (Since we were no longer her legal guardians, it would have to be a court commitment.) Then I said, "If you have any idea of what an institution for the insane can be like . . ." As I recall, she thought a minute, and kind of smiled, and said, "It was a good try." I said, "Why?" and she replied, "Well, if I'd been sent to the mental hospital, it would have been for just one month's observation. If I'd convinced them I was sane, then I'd have gotten out on probation."

Knowing what juvenile hall was like, the Bernards agree they couldn't blame anyone for trying any means to get out. "It even smells bad there," Priscilla says.

BOB: We just couldn't get Ellie's probation officer to take any positive action. Finally I put all the cards on the table. I told her either to get Ellie out or I'd be coming for her with legal help. We were told that there was no place to put her, that she was still way down on the waiting list. I found that hard to believe and decided not to wait any longer. So I said, "Let's start thinking about a private institution, and my hospitalization will cover it."

Within three weeks, Ellie was out of the juvenile hall environment and into a psychiatric hospital not far from the Bernard home.

6

A LONG TRIP HOME

BECAUSE OF A RESTRICTIVE VISITING ARRANGEMENT for new
patients, it would be almost six weeks before Ellie's
parents could see her at the hospital. But Ellie stayed
only four weeks. She and another girl climbed over the
fence late one summer night, and the Bernards did
not hear from their daughter again for six months—six
months to the day.

PRISCILLA: While she was in the hospital she really felt
we weren't interested, which is hard for us to understand. But I think she honestly felt that way.

BOB: This was *very* hard for us to understand, because we went down to the hospital every Wednesday

evening for parent group conferences, and every time we went we took her clothing and gifts so she would know that we were there and that we were thinking about her. Also, we were allowed to write to her, so of course we did so regularly.

PRISCILLA: But she had this idea that if we really cared about her, somehow or other she could be at home. And I think she felt we were buying her off, placating her.

However, that was apparently not the reason Ellie ran away again.

ELLIE: I was afraid the hospital was going to do shock treatments on me, because I'd heard this hinted around. Also, I'd heard they were going to keep me there for sixteen months. I just wasn't buying any of it.

PRISCILLA: All these reactions were the effect of us not being able to see her, to give her some reassurance.

So Ellie and her friend made their way to Santa Barbara, and Ellie subsequently went on alone to the Haight-Ashbury in San Francisco. (This was the time that her guitar and a number of her original compositions were stolen from her.)

ELLIE: This time I only spent one day in Frisco. And I hated it. It had just completely changed. It was so ugly—such a depressing sight. It was right at the time of the Haight Street riots, y'know? All my favorite shops had closed up. Six months before, I'd known everybody on Haight Street, and everybody knew me. Now I couldn't see anybody I knew. Like, in all the millions of people, I didn't see one familiar face.

So Ellie started thumbing and made her way up to
Seattle again, where she stayed about three weeks. Then
she went south again to Portland where she stayed, on
and off, for about three months. When not in Portland she
was at a commune she started not far from there.

In Portland she tried to "put down on," or give up the
use of methamphetamine, which was "her" trip. Known as
speed, it, along with the other amphetamines, is the sub-
ject of a slogan that straight society sometimes misreads:
Speed kills. She was, she frankly admits, a meth addict.

ELLIE: I was really tripping a lot. I was a speed freak.
But one of the cats I met was a good friend, and he
helped me to put down on speed.

But Ellie soon met another "cat" who got her back on
meth. Now both speeding and dealing heavily, Ellie
headed back to San Francisco, where she "tripped around
for a while." Finally, she put down on speed again. "I
just didn't have enough money to support my habit."
However, that too was only an interlude. It was not long
before she was speeding once more. Finally, the third
time she put down, she was ready to make it stick.

ELLIE: Then I put down because I dug myself too
much [had too much regard for herself] to see myself
getting messed up like that. When I was a meth freak
it just changed my whole disposition. I went from a
really friendly person, eager to help anybody, to a really
uptight person who was capable of stealing from her
best friend—y'know?—just to get some speed.

About the time she put down meth, Ellie began yearning to return to her home. But before she had run off

this time she had been warned by three different authorities (the hospital, juvenile hall, and her probation officer) that to violate her probation would mean a minimum of one year with the California Youth Authority—possibly in one of those barbed-wire-type camps in the mountains. At this point, she just wasn't ready to face that.

ELLIE: Though I got off meth, I was still dropping heavy psychedelics. Really heavy doses of it. And I dropped one night with my boyfriend, and he freaked out and beat me up. You know, just went crazy and was going to kill me. After that, I put down on psychedelics too.

Shortly after that incident Ellie hitchhiked to Santa Barbara, where she stayed for several weeks. By this time her physical system was showing the effects of its abuse. She had a severe bronchial infection and has since suffered attacks of nephritis, probably caused by a case of untreated strep infection that she must have had at that time.

While in Santa Barbara, she got word from a San Francisco friend that he had arranged a singing engagement for her in New Mexico. She decided to hitchhike to San Francisco to make further arrangements, then hitchhike around Arizona to New Mexico. ("You get busted real easy in Arizona.") But Ellie got only as far as Vallejo.

ELLIE: I was so sick I couldn't even stand up to hitchhike. So I made it to a bus depot and took a bus back to Frisco.

From there she called her father to come and get her.

ELLIE: I really wanted to put it all behind me. Like, I wanted to turn myself in for about three months prior to this time, but I just wasn't ready to go to jail. But I finally decided it would be worth it to get back home, no matter how long I had to be locked up. I don't know, I just knew I wasn't going to be happy until I was legal.

Ellie called her parents from San Francisco about four thirty on a Sunday afternoon: "I'm ready to come home." Her father took the next flight to San Francisco and had her back in Los Angeles by ten o'clock that night.

When she called, Ellie had one request of her parents: Could she spend one night at home before they notified the authorities? Worried about her health, they kept her home about a week before they finally had to call her probation officer to report that she was back.

As it turned out, Ellie did not have to be locked up, but, of course, she had had absolutely no prior way of knowing this. As far as she was concerned, she was coming home to spend a year in jail and get it over with.

7

"THE MODERN APHRODITE"

OBVIOUSLY Ellie is a very complex personality. To describe her background and her travels does not adequately describe her as a person. One quality that doesn't quite come across in such a run-through is her idealism, her almost passionate quest for that which has beauty.

Ellie is good evidence that even if your teen should display the "worst" of actions and decisions in his climb toward maturity, he may, even so, be made up of the more exquisite qualities of life.

Ellie's idealism is reflected in a poem she wrote shortly before her sophomore year, just as she was at the threshold of her runaway experiences. She entitled it "The Modern Aphrodite." Though she might not yet be able to recognize it, the poem seems to be talking about a part of Ellie herself—her dream for her own selfhood.

Eyes mystical, enchanting,
    Electrically charged with passion,
Wide with innocence, deep with love,
    Eyes that bespeak the soul, dominating
A face inconsequential in comparison,
    Nose a mere nose, ears hearing blasphemy,
But a mind that dismisses it,
    Bringing peace and tranquillity to prevail.

Hair streaming down in color cascades,
    Iridescent light to gleaming brown,
Shining with luster unbeheld by naked eye
    But comprehended by the bending mind,
Swirling, shimmering with rays of love.
    The skin pale with lightest blue translucence
Reflecting hair and eyes, basking in their glory
    Magically glowing under the dim worldly lights.

Body formed to perfection, voluptuous,
    Yet touched with the innocence of virginity,
Swerving, swelling, expounding radiant sensuality
    Unblemished every way, a human Aphrodite.
Most beautiful of all, the mind, learned is she,
    Learned in life but undestroyed by evil.
Optimistically she revels in the knowledge
    That beauty can never really be subdued.

Lacking suspicion, she knows not the webs
    Of lies hurled at humanity.
She has no name but that of love.

She is the perfect woman.
Her existence is only
In the tangles of my mind.

So, at not quite fifteen, Ellie wrote a hymn of praise to innocence and love, peace and tranquillity, beauty and truth. When she began running away only a few weeks later, she distorted this idealism, used it for her own purposes, tested its validity, and did not always live by it. But, at the end, her idealism remains still pretty well intact. Whatever else she did with it, she did not disclaim it. Looking back now, we can see a sort of prophecy in her words, ". . . learned is she, Learned in life but undestroyed by evil."

Of course Ellie was affected by the sordidness she lived in, but it is important for parents of other teens to recognize that she was not converted by it.

8
"LET'S DRAW BLOOD"

DURING THE TWO-YEAR SPAN of their family's ordeal, the Bernards reached out many times for professional help. They did not find it. Instead, they were insulted, accused, and browbeaten by counselors of both professional and self-appointed variety.

Their first experience was in northern California. After the time Ellie had run away and was gone overnight, the Bernards went to a counseling service available to families on a one-session basis. With Ellie present, they told a psychiatrist what had happened. The counselor then turned to Bob and asked, "What is the worst thing that you think could have happened to your daughter while she was gone?"

Bob replied, "Well, to my way of thinking, the worst thing that could have happened to her is that she could have been raped and murdered."

To which the counselor responded, "Well, she's going to die sometime, and if she lives a normal life, she is going to experience sex, so how can that be the worst thing that could happen to her?" If, in some remote way, that answer was designed to comfort or to reassure, it fell far short.

PRISCILLA: And he didn't stop there. He went on to say that Ellie's running away "is certainly not the worst thing your child is going to do." Which, of course, turned out to be true, but with Ellie, a mere fourteen years old, sitting there and hearing all this—

BOB: It could well have given her a little fuel. Another thing, the psychiatrist had absolutely no understanding of our concern that Ellie's friends were all so much older than she. So the whole conversation made us feel that we were completely undercut.

PRISCILLA: When we came out of there, even Ellie was rather shocked by what had been said. She could reject our authority, but to hear another authority do so was kind of jolting to her.

As it turned out, that session was one of the least distressing of the counseling experiences the Bernards were to have. The next experience was almost frightening in its implication of blackmail and ransom.

Though not pretending to be qualified psychiatrists, the Diggers Benevolent Society had apparently taken it upon themselves to aid and abet runaways and to advise their parents. The evening of the day Ellie had run away to Sunset Strip, her mother received a call from a woman at the Diggers.

PRISCILLA: She introduced herself as either a psychiatrist or a counselor—I forget which, but she had a title for herself. Her opening statement was, "I just wondered if you might be at all interested in where your daughter is." And she said it in about that snide tone of voice. Obviously, I was extremely interested in where my daughter was. The woman said she just wanted to be certain before she went any farther with the conversation.

Then she said that Ellie could be seen at the Diggers address in Hollywood. "But," she said, "don't notify the police." I told her that I had already done so, that Ellie was a missing person. She insisted I was to come down to the Diggers unescorted by anyone, especially the police.

I told her, "My husband is out of town, I've never driven on the freeway, and I'm shaking all over now. I don't think I could get down there in one piece unless I have a friend come with me." She allowed then that I could bring a friend, but the friend could not come into the room when I saw Ellie.

Those were the conditions I was to adhere to if I wanted to see my daughter. In fact, it was expressed in just that way: "Here are the conditions."

When we got to the address, I was taken into a room where I was introduced to this self-appointed counselor. He told me that when a runaway kid comes into the Diggers Society, the Diggers find out why the youngster ran away, then call the parents to come in. If they can get the parents and the child to agree as to conditions around the home, they advise the child to go home. But then he said, "Of course, if the conditions are not met by the parents, and the child runs away again, we will not tell you where she is." He said, in fact, "You will not see your child again." It was brutal. The whole thing was extremely brutal.

BOB: He also said, "We will put them in the underground."

PRISCILLA: Yes! He told me, "We can hide them out for days at a time. We have doctors and lawyers and other people who will help these kids, and house them for a couple of nights at a time."

BOB: It's like the old underground railroad: the kids are transported over to someone's house for a few nights, and then to someone else's. And if the police are getting a little close, then they send them up to San Francisco or down to San Diego, or wherever that same sort of thing is going on.

PRISCILLA: Now how much of this was actual fact, and how much was scare tactics, I don't know. But he was really convincing to me.

When Ellie came into the room, the "counselor" asked her what it was she wanted at home. What was the big reason why she had run away? What would keep her from running away again?

PRISCILLA: Ellie said she wanted complete freedom. He asked me if I were willing to give it to her. I said, "Of course not. She isn't even fifteen years old. Who can have complete freedom at any age, and particularly at that age?" So then he said, "Well, then, why should she come home?"

I remember saying to him, "That's emotional blackmail! Either I give this freedom, or you take my child."

Finally, after we talked back and forth, I agreed that depending on what concrete things she would like changed, I would consider whether I could morally or emotionally or mentally go along with them. So she came home with the idea that we would give it some talk for a few days. Bob spoke to her from Illinois that night, and we both said that we would be willing to give in somewhat, depending on what the reasons were. But as far as complete absence of rules, we could not go along with that. So then she was gone again the next morning.

Maybe it was a mistake. Maybe we should have promised her complete freedom, and hope she would become more sensible in a few days. But we didn't feel we could lie to her.

But maybe, too, if the "counselor" from the Diggers had not encouraged her, Ellie might have stayed home long enough to work out that particular crisis.

Bob flew home from Illinois that Saturday, and on the way home from the airport, the Bernards stopped at the Diggers to see if they could get a lead on Ellie's whereabouts. This time Priscilla waited in the car while Bob went in.

Bob: There was a very big thing—it wasn't blackmail that you could put your hands on, but it went like this: No, Ellie wasn't there, but they had a lot of connections, and they might be able to find her. But, boy, the bills were sure piling up, they couldn't pay their phone bill, and they just didn't know how they would find the money to do this good work of theirs.

So as I left, I gave them a five-dollar bill, and came on

with, "This is a wonderful organization you have here."
But it really tore me apart. I felt split down the middle
because I was supporting this dreadful work. But if
there were any chance that in their eyes I could come off
a good fellow and therefore one they might give some
bit of information to, then I had to go along with it. But
it was another kind of blackmail, almost like ransom:
Give us some money and you might get your child back.

For all of the Bernards' acceding to the Diggers Society, Ellie did not return there. Instead, she went to
one of the several churches in the Hollywood area that
minister to the hippie, runaway, and drug crowds.

Bob's reaction to the churches' approach to this ministry is one of utter opposition.

BOB: They are just a harbor for these kids. The
churches are prolonging the problem, supporting the
habit, rather than doing something to cut it off. The
kids go there and get food once or twice a day, and sleep
on the floor and in the yard at night. They don't have to
come home because their needs are easily taken care of.
I feel those set-ups are doing ten times more harm than
good.

PRISCILLA: The one church official we spoke to on
Sunset Strip really didn't seem terribly interested in our
problem. His attitude was that our child was just one of
the hundreds.

Q: Is there some sort of working relationship between
these churches and the Diggers?

BOB: No, it just so happens that the kids were har-
boring themselves at one place or the other. But we feel
the approach was the same in both places. For instance,

there was a bus system from one church going north. Somebody would be there with a car, and they would fill it up with runaways and haul them up north. A couple of days later, another car would be available.

PRISCILLA: Now, this was not under the auspices of the church, you understand, but it was happening there. And that was what really bothered us. Obviously if drugs are being peddled on the premises, if hippie wedding ceremonies are being performed there, if kids are making out sexually in vehicles on the church's parking lot, this is not with the approval of the church's members or their minister. But youngsters don't necessarily reason that way. Ellie expressed it to us, "How can it be so bad if it's going on at a church?" It seemed to us that the church officials there ought to be taking some responsibility for the attitude of these kids, because the youngsters will use whatever they hear, and whoever they meet there, to support their own actions. After all, "It's at a church."

So far, one professional psychiatrist, one self-appointed counselor, and at least one member of a church staff had been in a position to help provide a sense of direction for Ellie's parents. But their collective advice amounted to: Expect your daughter to do worse things than run away, and don't feel bad if she gets raped or murdered; give her complete freedom or we'll spirit her away on our underground railroad; and realize, please, that your daughter is only one of the hundreds.

BOB: Still we kept seeking help, trying to explore every avenue that was open. We went for one session to another family counseling service. But for some reason this counselor, a woman, took an extreme dislike to me—immediately.

PRISCILLA: Yes, it was very obvious.

BOB: And in the course of the conversation it came out that I had recently spanked Ellie. Ellie had gotten sassy with Priscilla one night, so I gave her a whack on the rear end. I said, "You don't talk to your mother like that." So—one whack.

When this came out, the counselor really turned on me. She said that it is never permissible to strike a child on any portion of the body, or with any degree of intensity after age three.

PRISCILLA: Up to that time, I guess it's supposed to be perfectly lovely!

BOB: And then this woman said, and I couldn't believe my ears, "How often do you hit your wife?"

PRISCILLA: We go there for help, and Bob gets castigated! Instead of help, it was, Let's throw blame. Someone's guilty; let's find out who. Meantime, here's Ellie, sitting there soaking all this stuff in. However, I think she thought it was sort of humorous, but I don't think the woman ever really got through to her, or even tried.

BOB: Finally the gal said, "I don't see any point in your coming back, because I don't think I can help you." Then, after insulting us and dismissing us as hopeless, the counseling service sent us a bill!

Whereas Bob caught the brunt of that counseling encounter, Priscilla's turn was coming, in an experience that left her shaken for months. Again it was a woman counselor, and again it was the idea of Find a culprit! Everything will be all right as soon as that person assumes the responsibility for all that has happened, and whips himself enough for it.

PRISCILLA: It probably took a year to get me over that experience. I was really *blamed*—for all that had happened. Totally and solely blamed. For some reason, right from the first visit, the counselor decided that I was the responsible person. Her questions seemed geared to expose in what area I was most responsible, what sins she could peg me with.

BOB: Priscilla was to blame because the counselor felt she was weak. The counselor actually goaded Ellie with her questions into saying that her mother was weak.

PRISCILLA: Also, the fact that I find it hard to be physically demonstrative with Ellie came out. But up to that point I thought I had been very *emotionally* responsive. And I know right now that I have been, and am. But this just really got to me—the idea that because my father never kissed me as a child, I am not demonstrative with Ellie, and therefore my child was on drugs!

I remember one time in particular that the counselor asked Ellie a question, and she just started crying. Bob and I felt all along that Ellie had been "covering," not reflecting her true feelings. We both felt these tears were a matter of cover-up, and perhaps confusion, because she couldn't think fast enough to say the "right" thing. So I just sat there. But Mrs. Kaufmann, the counselor, went over immediately, put both arms around Ellie, and looked at me and said, "Doesn't it ever occur to you to do this?" This was her whole reaction all the way along. So then of course I thought, Oh, *why* didn't it occur to me?

BOB: We finally stopped going there because Ellie

did not want to continue and we honestly did not feel it was doing any of us any good. In fact, it was producing a great deal of anxiety for Priscilla. In addition, it was a real financial burden, though that would not have been a consideration if there had been any positive results we could have pointed to.

Then, at Thanksgiving, within ten days after we stopped, Ellie took off again. About three weeks later, Mrs. Kaufmann called me at my office: "When are you going to start back on counseling?" I said, "There is no reason to, because Ellie has run away."

"Oh, my gosh," she says, "that's terrible. Oh, I must talk to you and your wife."

I refused, but she persisted. Finally she said, "I'll call you back in a day or so. In the meantime, you talk to your wife, and tell her that it's most important that I see you."

Mrs. Kaufmann placed the next call to Priscilla. But Priscilla was so upset she couldn't speak to her.

PRISCILLA: All she had to say was, "I'm Mrs. Kaufmann," and I just started weeping. I remember she said, "Come in to see me. I must help you." But I think I just said, "I can't," and hung up. I just could not have gone back into that atmosphere. I don't really know what her motives were in zeroing in on me. Maybe she wanted to get me to admit complete guilt so she could paste me back together again. But at that point, I just simply could not have taken any more of it.

BOB: We finally reached a level at which we rejected the whole idea of anyone being able to help us.

PRISCILLA: It was almost like an arena: Something's

happened, and someone's to blame, so let's draw blood! Never was it a matter of, What's important to this member of the family, or what's important to that one, and how can we work it out?

Factors behind the Bernards' being badgered by these counselors ranged from what was probably inept or misguided good intentions (on the part of the official at the Sunset Strip church) to possible ulterior motives (on the part of the Diggers) to a kind of overtraining (on the part of the psychiatrists).

Apparently the Bernards' psychiatrists were still tightly bound to the conventional school of psychiatry. Some branches of that school seem to lean heavily toward trotting out one's inadequacies, toward placing blame for one's failure on the experiences of the past, and toward the counselor's need to remain a cool, remote, uninvolved prodder.

A newer emphasis in psychiatry moves away from all those ideas. One example of it is reality therapy. A few years ago a young psychiatrist, Dr. William Glasser, began to reflect on his concern about the effectiveness of conventional psychiatry. As a result, he and Dr. G. L. Harrington developed what they call reality therapy. (Dr. Glasser explains reality therapy in a very readable book, *Reality Therapy*; Harper & Row, Publishers, Inc., 1965.)

The Bernards coincidentally assume Dr. Glasser's position when they say, "Though we don't feel Ellie should be blamed in a judgmental way (for after all, she was a child), nevertheless we get a bit incensed when counselors refuse to allow her to take responsibility for her own acts. We think we ought to be able to say, 'You have made a bad choice.' How else is she going to learn?" This is essentially the point of view of reality therapy.

A marvelous parody of the conventional psychiatric technique of visiting the sins of the *children* onto the *parents* unto the third and fourth antecedents is found in the musical drama *West Side Story*. Sung lustily by a gang of teen-age boys, part of it goes:

> Dear kindly Sergeant Krupke,
> You gotta understand
> It's just our bringin' up-ke
> That gets us outta hand.
> Our mothers all are junkies,
> Our fathers all are drunks.
> Golly Moses, natcherly we're punks!

Now if Sergeant Krupke had been a reality therapist, he might have responded:

> Dear kindly street gang members,
> You gotta understand
> It's *not* your bringin' uppers
> That gets you outta hand!
> Your mothers may be junkies,
> Your fathers may be drunks,
> But still *you* made the decision to be punks!

In other words, the emphasis is strictly on one's *present* ability to choose his own behavior, rather than on how someone else may have messed up one's *past*.

This realistic, accept-your-own-responsibility approach

is made bearable by the interrelationship between the counselor and the counselee. The counselee receives support in the form of acceptance and concern and even friendship from the counselor.

Up to this point, the Bernards had experienced none of this. Instead, they suffered unfair and uncalled-for debasement and anxiety, because other persons, not necessarily wiser and obviously not better, played "Who done it?" with their already raw emotions.

What does all this say to other parents of kids on drugs? Clearly, we would not discourage families from turning to any kind of psychiatric assistance that is truly helpful. But if, in the course of the counseling, any one member of the family is obviously and consistently being stripped of his sense of self-worth, the family needs to know that there is another option: You do not have to take that sort of counseling, nor do you have to struggle through crisis all alone. There *is* another, more supportive, more *effective* kind of help, because there *are* counselors who care more about other persons than about their inadequacies.

9

"WE WEREN'T ALL BAD"

AT A POINT at which the Bernards were thoroughly conditioned against counseling of any sort, their lives were touched by a pastor whose aim was to undergird and to reconcile rather than to blame. He is James A. Johnson, a minister of The United Presbyterian Church U.S.A. Much of Jim's highly creative energy throughout his ministry has gone into two emphases that would seem to have especially prepared him to be of help in a situation like that of the Bernards. They are the areas of working with young persons and of exploring with earnestness the counseling process.

Priscilla and Bob had begun attending services at the church in which Jim Johnson serves.

BOB: But we weren't going back to any more counselors.

PRISCILLA: By this time we were pretty negative about that.

They didn't have to go to Jim. He came to them.

PRISCILLA: We didn't even know Mr. Johnson except as a name on the Sunday bulletin. (The Sundays we had attended that church, one of the other ministers preached.) But he phoned and introduced himself and said he'd been told that our daughter was in juvenile hall.

MR. JOHNSON: The church staff had heard that a family who was new in our church had a girl in juvenile. I don't think we even knew what the trouble was.

PRISCILLA: He said he wanted to explain that this kind of thing had happened before to other members of the congregation, and that as a minister he could visit juvenile hall anytime during the week. Did we think our daughter would be interested in having another weekly visitor?

This was our first contact with him, and it was in the nature of, I want to do something to help, to make someone feel a little better. It wasn't, Who did it? Or, Why did it happen? It was just, Here I am; would she like a visitor?

The first time around, the answer was no. Ellie refused to see Jim.

BOB: For one thing, she didn't know who he was. Also, she was rejecting anything in the nature of the Establishment, including the church.

PRISCILLA: It was like she wanted everyone in authority to be against her, because this would give her an excuse for her behavior.

BOB: So we let it go until we could see her again ourselves. Then we explained that Jim Johnson had not given up, that he was still willing to come down. "We can only see you forty-five minutes on a Sunday afternoon. His visit would give you a chance to talk to somebody else during the week, to break the routine a bit."

Thereafter, Mr. Johnson went down to juvenile hall once a week during Ellie's long, unhappy stay there. After each visit, he called her parents to report on her general condition.

MR. JOHNSON: Sometimes I could see that nothing much had seemed to happen through my visit. There were days I didn't think I'd done a thing by going down, outside of the fact that I'd demonstrated that I cared enough to come.

But that seems to be all that was necessary at that point, for in retrospect, Ellie says, "It was really a big help, knowing that somebody I hadn't even known before could care."

But when Ellie was transferred to the psychiatric hospital, she was temporarily allowed no visits, not even from the minister. And then she went A.W.O.L. again.

Her parents began to turn to Mr. Johnson, as a friend, for some personal help. Bob called Jim and asked for an appointment around the time of Ellie's sixteenth birthday. Besides his great worry over Ellie, he had the added tension of a job change to deal with.

Bob: We talked for an hour or more. And I came out feeling a great deal of reassurance. I guess I needed somebody to say I was O.K. too. And the opportunity to have him pray with me was a new kind of experience.

Later, just before Christmas, the Bernards went to Mr. Johnson together. They had planned to visit Priscilla's parents over the holidays. They had no reason to expect to hear from Ellie. She had been gone well over five months with no word at all. Also, she had spent the previous Christmas away from home. However, according to Bob, "I guess we both got guilt feelings about leaving without knowing where she was."

Priscilla: It was a big thing at the time for either of us to deliberately seek out help after the counseling experiences we'd gone through. But with Jim, it was never a question of blame; it was just, This is how things are right now; where do you go from here?

Bob: He gave us an awful lot of reassurance of Ellie as a person, as not being hopeless.

Priscilla: He said, "Sure, it's not the sort of life you would have picked for your child. But she's got a strong enough ego so that she'll only go so far, and then she'll stop and say, 'But I'm Ellie Bernard; I can't do this.'" His feeling was that this inner strength would eventually save her, that she just didn't have suicidal tendencies in terms of taking her own life (which we had worried about), nor in terms of throwing it away, wasting it.

Bob: There was also a great deal of reassurance to *us* as persons, that what we were doing was right. His recognizing us as individuals, with individual problems, was important to us. We found out we weren't all bad.

MR. JOHNSON: One of the good things that happened was that the Bernards began to accept *themselves*. In spite of what happened to Ellie, they weren't just big fat failures in life.

PRISCILLA: He helped us see that whereas something is right for one person in terms of response and behavior, it might not be right for another. As Mrs. Kaufmann kept reminding me, I am not a physically demonstrative person, and I probably never will be. But Mr. Johnson pointed out that there are lots of ways you show your love to your children. They can't just hang you with the idea that because you don't run up to them ten times a day and throw your arms around them, "Mama doesn't love me," while meantime Mama is reading to them or playing games with them, or doing something else that is showing the same sort of love.

BOB: That session with Jim really sort of put us back together again.

MR. JOHNSON: I get tears in my eyes when I think about that session, because that was going to be a very difficult Christmas for Priscilla and Bob. I remember asking the staff to be praying about my conference with the two of them. They came into my study anxious and sad and hurting. And dreading the upcoming Christmas holiday without Ellie. When they left, they were released and freed from the heaviness of the burden. It was as obvious as if all of a sudden the clouds had rolled back and the sun was shining. I remember feeling that the Holy Spirit had more to do with that one than I did. He really gave me the things to say.

Jim Johnson's understanding of the work of the Holy Spirit is not of the "I have an exclusive pipeline to the Lord" ilk. Instead he says: "God is an active agent down in the nitty-gritty of *all* of our lives. I strongly believe, for instance, that even when the parent is not there to oversee the life of a runaway youngster, the Holy Spirit *is* there."

This kind of faith gives another dimension—intuitiveness—to the concept of trust. Realistic trust—plus *faith* —becomes intuitive trust. This is not a reference to the kind of intuition that is lightly referred to as women's intuition and is supposed to detect a husband's otherwise well-kept secrets. Nor is it a reference to the kind of intuition that is associated with extrasensory perception and causes faraway events to "inbreak" onto a person's consciousness. But it *is* to speak of the knowledge of some secret, some truth of creation that is not provable by reasoning, and that can be perceived only by the eyes of faith.

In this case, intuitive trust has its base in the faith that the Creator who gave us the gift of life *still cares*, and is constantly calling, calling us back into relationship with his purpose for our lives.

It was out of this kind of trust that Jim Johnson could say to the Bernards: "I believe that God deals with each individual in terms of where he is and what he is going through. Now, you built a lot of values into Ellie through the years. I'm convinced these values won't be lost. You have to trust a kind of inner wisdom in such a person as Ellie to finally sort things out."

Because intuitive trust is partly realistic trust, it allows for wrong decisions and recognizes that those wrong decisions don't have to be the end of the world for a teen-ager. Intuitive trust knows the youngster can, and probably will, come back.

MR. JOHNSON: The framework of any situation is never so important as what's happening to the persons involved. Sometimes a youngster will seek out the experiences he has to have. We have to learn to trust the soul to respond to those experiences with growth.

Priscilla believes that one must also recognize that a youngster may ultimately make it through, come back from his predicament, even though he may not come back home.

PRISCILLA: His making it through may not depend so much on what we can give him now as it does on what we have given him in the past.

MR. JOHNSON: Sometimes parents have to accept the right of the child to be responsible for his own life at an earlier age than the parent would wish.

Intuitive trust also has about it a quality of healing. The Bernards were healed of a great deal of their anxiety and a great deal of their self-doubt when they began to understand intuitive trust. And that served, in a large sense, as their preparation for Ellie's homecoming, which occurred less than a month later. They could now receive her more fully, more forgivingly, because her actions no longer meant that they were failures.

Of that preparation, sentimental trust would say, "What a lovely coincidence!" But intuitive trust knows differently. It can say with joy, and with the giving of thanks, "What a loving Providence!"

10
SOME SELFISH PERSONS

AS WITH ALL SOCIAL ILLS, the cure for the drug problem is thought by some to lie in legislation. Legislate to stop the stream of drugs into this country. Legislate to make "pushing" impracticable. Legislate to stop illicit manufacturing. Legislate to enforce legislation.

But the process of changing the system by law can be clumsy, backward, and sluggish. And the longer an issue is protracted, the more thousands of valuable lives may be devastated.

However, there is a much simpler, more direct, and infinitely more perfect alternative for change available for any social ill. But too terribly often it is abhorred by the decision makers involved. It is, simply, the choice to operate from a base of unselfishness. It is the *choice to consider other persons' well-being more sacrosanct, less expendable, than one's own drive for wealth or power, pleasure or acclaim.* To make that choice for unselfishness is the only real way (and it *is* a real way) one person can have immediate, positive effectiveness in dealing with a social evil.

However, selflessness involves an urgent concern, a love, for each other as sharers in the gift of life—and we humans, even we who claim to be followers of Christ, have refused outright to become a genuine family of man. At best we are content with or even bent on being merely a collection of busy and competitive neighbors. One begins to understand original, or corporate, sin: we have fallen short of God's aim for us; we have cheated ourselves of the creativeness of caring.

In the current drug crisis of our society, responsible, unselfish decisions can be made by caring people, individual people, to *substantially* diminish the problem. In more personal terms, such decisions could affect young lives directly, individually, redemptively.

For starters, there is our responsibility to care about what happens in each other's lives. One sixteen-year-old, Larry, was able to survive on a runaway excursion because he was taken in by the men's dorm on the campus of a small graduate school. One of the men there said he'd never seen anyone take so much speed as Larry did. He was a sick and messed-up boy. Now eighteen, Larry sporadically attends a discussion group for drug-attracted teens. In one of the discussions, he told about his experiences on the campus. He bragged, "I lived there and was selling $300 worth of stuff a week to those guys."

commercial drug companies operating within the law are too much a part of a system to change quickly—except, of course, by that deliberate choice for unselfishness! One authoritative estimate is that American drug companies legally produce three or four times more quantities of drugs than are needed for legal use, and that nine out of ten of all legally produced drug units find their way to illegal use.

American pharmaceutical companies can, and assuredly do, legitimately export quantities of their products to Mexico. American kids can, and assuredly do, legitimately cross the border in an afternoon's drive and legitimately purchase those same pills by the thousands. The only illegal part of the whole transaction is that the buyer turns smuggler to get the pills back into the States. And that's apparently not too hard to do.

ELLIE: You can buy pills by the jarful in any drugstore in Mexico. A jar costs about twenty-five dollars and has a thousand pills in it. You put them in rolls of , sell them for a dollar each, and you make seventy- bucks profit. [A jar, incidentally, is a unit of meas- Usually the thousand pills are packaged in paper instead of glass jars.]

then, by operating within the law, the drug com- can willfully—and legitimately—defeat the good of the law! Whatever happened to Paul's plea live by the *spirit* of the law, not by the letter

ally ironic is the fact that the companies in- e ostensibly dedicated to bettering the health d. Perhaps the president of each drug company

The kids of one accord landed on him. "You had a responsibility to those students, Larry." "A dealer always runs a big risk of messing someone up." "You should care more about people, Larry."

Larry responded: "To the people I sold to I feel no responsibility. They were doing postgraduate work. If they don't know where their heads are by this time, or if they don't know where they're at, why should I know where I'm at?"

The attitude of the other students was commendable, of course. But Larry's reply, immature and uncaring though it was, does have a certain logic to it. At least it raises the astounded question, Why didn't those postgraduate students care enough about that stoned sixteen-year-old boy to try to reclaim him?

It's true some tried to counsel him about his troubles, and apparently one student lost so much time because of Larry that his grades began to slip. But all the while this was going on, that physically dissipated, bombed-out minor was able to sell an enormous amount of speed to innumerable adult postgraduates, and even he knew they should have known better.

Those men were in a strategic position to make a responsible difference in that boy's life. But instead, they merely *used* him to further their own pleasurable interests in drugs. That's selfishness—the kind that counts regrettably in the shaping of lives.

(This example of the postgraduate students also typifies the fact that heavy drug use in America is not at all restricted to teens. One experienced social worker, in a conversation about teens on drugs, remarked solemnly, "Somebody ought to tell their parents to put down too.")

The whole question of where young dealers get their stuff is acutely illustrative of the kind of selfishness that moves our society. Illegitimate drug sources all have a common motivation: greed.

There are, for instance, bootleg drug factories that turn out diet-type pills to the same formula as the drug companies do. They can make them cheaply, and so kids can also buy them comparatively cheaply. But the huge quantity sold guarantees a wealthy bootlegger. It also all but guarantees a drug habit for a number of our teen-agers.

In one year alone recently, 102 such illegal garage-type laboratories were closed down across the country by the former Bureau of Drug Abuse Control. Now the Federal Bureau of Narcotics and Dangerous Drugs keeps an alert ear to the ground for information leading to these bootleg factories, though of course there is no way of knowing how many are operating at any one time.

The point that damns these bootleggers is the fact that there is absolutely no reason-for-being for them, except to gorge—by choice!—on the tragedy of others.

There is another, more respectably cloaked source, one that authorities don't seem to consider major. But we mention it here because it keeps cropping up in conversation with kids. Ellie is among those who claim that some youngsters get doctors to give them prescriptions for diet pills, and then they sell the pills, or use them to get high.

A check with a reputable doctor suggests that this is at least a possibility. He felt that some doctors may be so concerned with satisfying the whims of their clientele that they become casual and indiscriminate in prescribing

the medicine that the patient requests. Witness the so-called fat doctors, whose promiscuity in pill-dispensing was so thoroughly exposed as quackery in one of the major magazines a year or two ago. They got fat and rich while some of their patients got thin and "high."

Even legitimately given, prescribed pills can have disastrous results. A recent television commentary relate that an eleven-year-old girl, a confirmed drug addi got her start with prescribed diet pills when she only nine years old. (H'mmm, *nine* years old? One wonder, on second thought, just how legitimat prescription might be!) At any rate, shortly th the pills gave her the confidence to run away fr and now, at eleven, she is out on her own with a middle-aged man.

Another thing—even though the doctor r diet pills only with the greatest of care, possibility. Some young dopers alter the prescription, or renew it on a sheet fr scription pad. Obviously, this is the and not the doctors'. But it adds view of all these problems, is ther prescribe diet pills for young, firs weight by ingesting less food rat still be a viable option for them have no right to mess up a l with chemicals before the pa by taking in fewer calories.

Probably the largest an source of pills available most frustrating to deal out, individual docto

involved should voluntarily assume the responsibility of seeing for himself how effective is his work. Were these presidents to stroll up and down Sunset Strip on a Saturday night, for instance, they would see, on one corner, a girl squatted down against a building, alternately laughing hysterically and mumbling some indistinguishable word over and over. Other kids mill around, paying no attention at all, as if she were a figment of her own imagination and nobody else could see her.

The presidents would see another girl go up to an adult tourist and say, "Gimme a dime!" She stands there so aggressively he is taken aback and gives it to her. They would see one extremely thin, very long-haired boy with skin that is almost translucent pop three reds (depressants) in quick, open-view succession.

If those presidents stood at any one corner long enough, they would see, time after time, one youngster or another take a roll of money from his pocket, peel off a bill or two, and appear to just hold it. The presidents would not be as apt to see the money change hands. But they would shortly see the same kids tilting back their heads and popping in a pill in the closed-fist fashion one uses to toss in peanuts.

The presidents can, if they are observant, spot the weekend hippies as opposed to the runaway addicts. The weekenders may have the hair and the beards, but they also usually have clean clothes, which are often fairly Establishment-type. Some even have creases in their pants. Also, the weekenders are generally wearing shoes.

The addicted kids look terrible. That is, they look like they feel terrible. Their hair is matted, their faces have lines that swing from the corner of the eye down to the middle of the cheek, their eyes are red, their skin is pasty.

The addicts are not just here and there among the throng. Instead, there are many of them. And perhaps their most distinguishable characteristic is their sad demeanor. There is no joy in their faces, no youthful zest, no spontaneity. And there is no spring to the way they carry themselves, hands in pockets, shoulders hunched. To emphasize this kind of eerie sadness there is, strangely, a sort of sweetness to many of the kids, a sort of considerateness of the adult tourist who has ventured into this foreign territory, that makes one want to touch these kids gently and heal them of their affliction.

One wonders if these presidents of drug companies would be moved by what they see. Might they realize that their own sons and daughters are very liable to this same kind of physical sickness and mental unreality? And that they, their fathers, *have the power* to prevent such disaster for their children and for the children of those who do not have that kind of power?

But there is some evidence to indicate that these presidents and their fellow executives may not be capable of that kind of compassion, for *it isn't as if they have been unaware of what they are doing!* They know exactly what they are doing: they *know* they are risking our children's well-being for their own purposes. Neither Congressional investigation nor proposed law has caused them to back off.

Some authorities feel that their lack of compassion and of cooperation is economically based. That's a polite way of saying that the drug companies involved like the money they get from our kids more than they like our kids.

Other officials feel there is in the whole thing a great deal of the general resistance of industry to governmental control. In other words, some drug companies of America choose to sacrifice public interest (that is, they choose to put our youngsters' health on the line) for the monumentally selfish reason of maintaining the industry's prestige: Nobody's going to tell *them* what to do!

In our busy, competitive neighborhood, the decision makers strike again!

11
"IF THIS IS THE HIPPIE WORLD..."

ELLIE'S REEVALUATION of her offbeat way of life was a gradual process. First, she put down on speed because she didn't like what it was doing to her. Later, she put down on psychedelics because a boyfriend freaked out on them and tried to kill her.

Also, she was feeling a real sense of boredom.

ELLIE: You keep taking that stuff and you start getting bored. Nothing really looks that good to you anymore.

But it was the experience of living in the commune she started in Oregon that caused her to begin to take another look at the attitude of her hippie friends. She and another girl had been given permission by the owner, a young man whom she had befriended in Portland, to use a piece of property as a commune.

ELLIE: The property was a hundred acres, right in the middle of a rain forest. There were lots of pine trees, and a creek in front of the house that flowed into a river in back of the house. It was really beautiful. There were three cabins, shacks really. We turned one into our main cabin, one into an outhouse, and one into a bunkhouse.

The first time we went out to see it, about forty people went with us. About thirty-eight of them left the next day, when they saw how much work there was to be done! But we finally got it looking presentable, and it really made us happy when the cops came down and said, "You people are really doing a good thing out here, and we'll do anything we can to help you."

Strangely, that incident, that bit of approval and appreciation from the most straight of the Establishment, stands out for Ellie as a highlight in her journey away from home.

Hippies soon began arriving at the commune because Ellie had posted a notice in a crash pad in Portland. At one point there were as many as fifty people on the premises. Other times, Ellie was entirely alone.

ELLIE: I got so I loved it when I was alone, because the people that came there drove me crazy most of the time. I never saw such a bunch of people! We had some of these guys—big, able-bodied men, y'know? And all they'd do is lie around all day long while this other chick and I would go out and chop logs. And if you asked the guys to do something, like get a pail of water, they'd practically go insane: "Yes, sir!" "Yes, sergeant!" "Yes, commander!" You know, with the fake salute. They

were just so against work of any sort. And they drove
me crazy, because you *know* that they were the first
ones in line for food. They took the biggest helpings,
even if it meant that somebody else didn't get any. And
they always had the best beds in the place because they
never left them!

So the hippie way of life, at least as it was lived at
this particular commune, scored no points with Ellie.

And there was another incident at the commune that
also disgusted her.

ELLIE: On Friday nights, all the juicers from town
used to come out to the commune with their beer. One
night they got the guys of the commune so drunk that
most of them passed out. There were three of us chicks
living there at that time, and only about two of the guys
weren't drunk. One of them was a guy we called Scorpio
Dave. He was like the guru of the commune. The other
was a sixteen-year-old runaway. But these guys from
town were like in their twenties and thirties, and they
started making passes at us. I guess since we looked like
hippies they thought we must believe in free sex instead
of free love. But the three of us chicks were pretty big
and pretty strong, and we finally managed to escort
them out.

But I was really uptight—y'know?—because I thought,
O.K., where are the guys? You know, the guys are supposed to protect us. But my boyfriend's passed out from
being too drunk, another guy's throwing up all over the
place, and so forth. So I looked at Scorpio Dave and I
said, "Well, you're a man. Why didn't you protect us?"

So he sort of drawled, "Oh, just let them do their own
thing."

I said, "Well, wait a minute, man. I don't care if they do their *own* thing, but they're not gonna do it with me!"

So he says, "Well, you're just being uptight. You're really being uptight. They're just doing their own thing. I wasn't going to fight with them. We should all just get together."

Well, now the hippie philosophy is beautiful, but it can be carried to extremes, y'know? When I need help, I want my friends to help me. I don't want them to say, "Oh, that's O.K., if someone wants to kill you, that's his own thing. So what if you die?" Stuff like that I just can't handle.

After the commune folded, Ellie had yet another disappointment with her hippie friends. Some of the people that had lived at the commune got a house in Portland, and Ellie hoped to be able to stay there with them.

ELLIE: But they just said, "Sorry, you can't stay at our house because the cops might find out you're a runaway and bust us." That really made me feel bad, because I had just about solely supported them for a good three months. When they lived at my commune I did all the cleaning there, and all the cooking. I went to the city and "dealt" so we could have some money. I even went out and speared salmon in our river! I did all these insane things just to keep these people fed. Then when I needed some help, it was just, "Forget you."

There was one other incident, a more positive one, that had a bearing on Ellie's increasing desire to return from her "far country." She had met some married couples who were hipsters—but they had jobs, and nice homes, and "bookshelves full of really fantastic books."

ELLIE: When I finally decided to come home, I was at an all-time low. I was completely fed up with most of the people I'd met, and I was fed up with the state of mind I was in, with being just a doper. I was also fed up with the way my body was reacting to everything I was putting it through, because I was sicker than a dog. And I said, "Well, if this is the hippie world, forget it." My married friends had shown me that you don't have to have long hair to be a hipster. They were middle-class, respectable hipsters. And I decided that's what I wanted to be.

I think other kids will come back for the same basic reasons I did, y'know? They'll get to feeling they are selling out the other way. It's like you're taking the easy way out, by not ever doing anything very responsible. That way of life gets real boring.

When other kids do begin to yearn for home, they may or may not be dependent upon their parents to get them there. And if they are, their parents may or may not be willing to go that extra mile.

MR. JOHNSON: Thank God the Bernards had maintained the kind of relationship with Ellie in which she could feel free to call them when she wanted them. I think that's a real tribute to what her parents were through this, and to what they did: they could leave her feeling comfortable enough to call. And it apparently never occurred to Ellie that her dad would do anything else but hop the next plane and come and get her, which he did. So the message they got over was a very clear one, and it was very good: they had not rejected her.

12

A LITTLE TEST
FOR US "STRAIGHTS"

CHECK WHICH YOUR REACTION HAS BEEN, or would be, to the following situations. We trust you (probably sentimentally!) to be honest.

Situation 1. You must lose twenty pounds.

_____A. Do you rigidly, strictly, steadfastly, relentlessly stick to your diet—without ever weakening, not even once?
_____B. Or, do you stick to your diet pretty well, but break it occasionally when social nicety is involved (such as when a hostess encourages you to have one more of her specialty)?

————C. Or, do you get *so* hungry after a few days on a diet that eventually you settle for knocking off a half pound this week, and you'll "try again after the holidays"?

Situation 2. You left your mate a week ago. Now you are ashamed.

————A. Do you return, admit you were wrong, and try to start over?

————B. Or, do you come back making excuses for yourself?

————C. Or, do you find it easier not to come back at all?

Situation 3. You cheated on your income tax in a large but clever way. Conviction will mean a jail sentence. It isn't likely you'll ever be found out, but still you've had some sleepless nights.

————A. Do you turn yourself in, pay your debt to society, and pick up the threads of your life from there?

————B. Or, do you choose not to face going to prison, but you still continue to agonize over it?

————C. Or, do you just shrug the whole thing out of your mind?

Well, now, how did you check out? If you chose answer A in every situation, then you must be such a paragon of self-discipline that you probably would never find yourself in those kinds of situations in the first place! Which may be very good, except that it isn't likely then that you will ever understand the human predicaments more mortal-type people fall into.

If, on the other hand, you know what it is to be socially pressured into ingesting something that you know you shouldn't—

Or if you know what it is to have an emotional dependency on such a thing as food (or with some people it's cigarettes or liquor or, uh, drugs)—

Or if you've ever had to admit that you were seriously and tragically wrong—

Or if you've ever had to choose between your conscience and your freedom—

—then you can begin to understand the great struggle your youngster must go through when he begins wanting to rise above his own private little mire.

And if, by any chance, you checked even one answer C, then you should have gotten a glimpse of the kind of determined *courage* your youngster must gather up in order to come back home. This is especially true if he will have to face serious consequence.

When your youngster is ready to make that decision to return, it will be because he has gained some insight that tells him there is a better way of using up his life.

MR. JOHNSON: But parental anxiety can rob him of that insight. Parents so often get in the way of a kid's learning. By saying, "I told you so!" or by preaching at the youngster, or by rescuing him too quickly from the consequences of his own actions, the parent robs him of the fruit of his experience. When that happens, the youngster may have the need to repeat the experience until the lesson is his own.

A good place to begin respecting the youngster's insight is to take seriously his maturity in deciding to

come back. Chalk up one for his side for making that
future-altering decision. At the very least, to do so makes
a better starting point for a new relationship than holding
over him the idea that he shouldn't have gone in the
first place.

In Ellie's particular situation, there was a poignancy
that did not escape her parents. There was an irony to
the fact that Ellie's good decision to return to normal
society was to be rewarded by a year in jail. At the time
she placed the phone call to her parents, she was absolutely certain that she was on her way to the California
Youth Authority.

PRISCILLA: There was no choice, as far as she was
concerned. If she wanted to get back to some form of
normal life, she had to get that year in prison out of
the way.

When she arrived home ill, the Bernards could not
bring themselves to call her probation officer until Ellie
had begun to respond to their care. Then, when she was
better, they went down for a hearing. The fact that
Ellie had come home voluntarily, in spite of the im-
pending jail sentence, worked heavily in her favor. But
also, in the meantime, the Bernards had been in close
contact with Jim Johnson. He volunteered to go with
them to the hearing, and offered to stand in the place of
Ellie's probation officer for regular counseling.

PRISCILLA: I'm quite sure that this made a considerable difference. The public defender seemed quite impressed with the fact that Mr. Johnson had taken the
trouble to be there.

Not to be underrated, though, is the fact that in spite of all the hassle of the two years past, Bob and Priscilla wanted their daughter home, and they sensed that they could now trust her decision to go straight.

With all these factors going for Ellie, the authorities decided not to "place" her. She was put on strict probation, of course. But she could live at home.

And so, for Ellie, there began a year of catching up. There were weekly conferences with Jim Johnson, enrollment in continuation school, employment as a receptionist and counselor at the local drug center, and, of course, the process of getting reacquainted with, and making adjustments within, the circle of her family.

13

AN EVENING
AT "THE GATEWAY"

SHORTLY AFTER ELLIE'S RETURN HOME, citizens concerned about the drug problem in that community arranged for the funding of a center to which youth could go for help.

From each of the district's schools, at least one youngster who had put down on drugs was asked to be on the organizing committee. Ellie was the only youngster in her school who had managed to stay clean. (Continuation school is not noted for its finesse. Youngsters are placed there who have missed regular schooling for one reason or another related to their behavior.)

Ellie not only helped with the planning of the drug center, which was named The Gateway, but she also became its secretary-receptionist and a sort of junior counselor.

On a summer night one can walk into the center (and anyone would be welcome) and find a scene almost resembling a stereotype of what a struggling youth center looks like. The major area is a big, barren, barnlike room with a scuffed wooden floor. There are several shoddy sofas and a couple of ping-pong tables, but they hardly make a difference to the emptiness of the room. A boxed set of Tolkien books rests on the arm of one of the sofas.

On another sofa, in the middle of the room, lies a young man sound asleep. He looks very weary, almost sick. He is wearing blue jeans that are covered with large splotches of paint. He is bare from the waist up. (And also from the ankle down!)

One of the center's counselors says the boy has no place to live at the moment and is staying with various friends a few days at a time. At nineteen, he is estranged from his parents who live in the area, close-by.

Most of the decor in the room is "Contemporary Message." On one side of a portable blackboard, someone has carefully printed, "One generation abandons the enterprises of the other like stranded vessels. —Henry David Thoreau from *Walden*." On the reverse side are these messages: "Think that you can know, and know that you cannot," and "But he is a friend that you can trust, and this is much in these days."

On the walls are various black-and-white photo posters. One is a picture of the real Bonnie Parker, cigar in mouth, gun in hand. Another shows Stokely Carmichael bundled in a pointed sweat-shirt hood. His hand is raised. And yet another poster shows one of Hollywood's sex symbols, possibly Brigitte Bardot, walking on a beach in a very teeny weeny bikini. There is also a piece of serious art, an oil painting of a black man, head raised, eyes closed. Under it, thumbtacked just casually enough so that it's hard to tell whether it is supposed to be related to the painting, is the crayoned sign, "And life is sweet."

Youngsters come and go freely during the evening. The programming, though structured, is relaxed. Those who do not wish to participate directly may play ping-pong or table games, or they may just sit and talk.

COUNSELOR: A lot of kids say, "There's nothing to do around here, so we take drugs." We hope to show them that straight relationships can be creative and fun.

The regular evening programs may consist of socio-drama, or sensitivity-type groups, or simply open-discussion groups. At least one night a week the center focuses on helping parents.

COUNSELOR: The philosophy of this place is nonjudgmental. We try to give the kids as much info as we can about drugs. One of our concerns is the number of kids who come in who really don't know the effects of some of the drugs. We cull some of the already printed stuff and put out our own material. Too much of the other is inaccurate and relies mostly on fear. Somebody is really trying to put the fear of something into these kids. Our approach is to try to start kids thinking about who they are and what drugs are doing to them.

Of the twenty or more kids in the room, only two, both boys, are wearing shoes. Ellie has on a long gown or muumuu of paisley print. Her feet are not totally bare —she has on a toe ring with a bell that tinkles as she moves about. Most of the girls are in blue jeans. Only one has on feminine, printed pants—two, counting a woman counselor. Most of the girls have straight, long hair. Surprisingly, there is only one boy with shoulder length hair. (Oops, scratch that! It's a girl!)

At the right moment in the evening, sofas are pulled into a circle at one end of the room, and a couple of counselors, including Ellie, invite the kids to join them for an open discussion. Twelve or fifteen youngsters come over. In an aside, Ellie explains to visitors: "All the kids here come in because they are willing to participate. Just coming in the door is a big step toward putting drugs behind them. Just getting them in is a big step toward getting them back into society."

But getting them in has some unexpected obstacles.

COUNSELOR: Many parents will not let their kids come to the center very often because they figure it will interfere with their homework. So the kid goes into his room, locks the door, and lights up a marijuana. Not too much is gained.

As the open discussion gets under way, conversation comes around to the topic of police. (The local police, incidentally, have agreed not to drop by The Gateway at all.) Ellie is reminded of an incident that occurred during one of her runaway excursions.

ELLIE: The first time I lived in Haight, I lived in this pad with a lot of other people. There was this big bag of garbage that nobody wanted to take out. So I looked out the window and saw two cops on the sidewalk below,

and I threw it out at them. We looked down and saw
the cops surrounded by garbage. When they started up
the stairs everybody in the pad hit for the closets. I
made myself presentable and answered the door: "Can
I help you?"

"Do you know anything about a bag of garbage?"

"No, sir, sorry I can't help you."

When the cops went back down, somebody in the pad
filled a plastic bag with water and dropped it down on
them. It went on that way all evening.

The story had momentum, and everybody laughed.
Ellie laughed, too, quite heartily. But when the spontaneity of the humor had subsided, an almost pained
expression flashed across her face.

ELLIE: I don't know why I thought it was so funny. I
hate it like at love-ins when guys do things like that. You
get in a group and someone yells an insult to a cop, and
the cops get uptight and everybody gets uptight and it's
no good.

Further in the discussion, the conversation focuses on a
young man, Dave, who had been terribly addicted to
meth. He had been placed for two months in a center
for special problems in the San Francisco area. "It was
either that or jail."

He was still greatly incensed, and even still feeling
quite sorry for himself, because the doctors had forced
him to eat.

DAVE: Physically, I have a body, and I can do anything I damn well please with it. The doctor didn't
know I just about flipped out when he came in with

that syringe. It took a lot of guts and courage for me to stay there. I kept writing on the wall and on paper, "Leave me alone. I'll eat when I'm ready." But they kept at me. They'd make me eat. What kind of doctors are those who, if you don't want to eat at twelve, make you eat?

In this atmosphere where loving acceptance is the key watchword, one could see the adult counselor's mind carefully formulating an honest but gentle answer. Ellie's youth was her strength at this point. She could be honest and not so gentle, and somehow, because she and Dave were peers, there seemed to be no rancor in her practical words.

ELLIE: Maybe they are doctors with fussbudget help— doctors who have got dishwashers who want to go home at twelve thirty. I think you are selfish, Dave.

DAVE: I think I am too, O.K. But the point is, I would have eaten if I'd been given my own time.

COUNSELOR: Are you aware when you are hungry when you are on meth?

DAVE: Not on meth, no.

ELLIE: Well, look, Dave, at least you got fed. Look at the bright side of it.

Ellie's practical side "gave it" to Dave once more before the evening was over. Dave was expounding his philosophy of life like an oracle of truth and wisdom. He concluded by saying, "If I can better myself through a particular situation, and if I can help even just five individuals, and they can help five others—"

ELLIE: Sounds like a chain letter—and they never work!

In talking to the visitors, Ellie said, "If one of the kids lies, we just say, 'Hey, guy, you're not telling us the truth. We like you and we want you to level with us.' I started that. I just don't like anyone to lie to me."

However astute Ellie is in this kind of discussion, she is, after all, younger than many of the kids who are there for counseling. She could not, and should not have to, suddenly become a full-time adult. Once during that discussion one of the adult counselors turned to Ellie and said, "Do you have anything to say about that point, Ellie?" Ellie said, "No," and the counselor responded, "You know why, don't you?" It was obvious that she meant that Ellie had forgotten her role as counselor, in a minor lapse into being a teen-ager: she and a young man were for the moment paying more attention to each other than to the discussion.

The work experience at The Gateway has sharpened Ellie's understanding of the tragedy of drugs. An old friend of hers came into the center one evening. He was showing no sign of recovering from his addicted way of life, and Ellie's compassionate nature was touched. She later said to her mother: "He has so much promise, so much intelligence. But he's lost. He's not only lost to himself, but to society. And we need people like him."

As graduation from continuation school and the prospect of entering college came upon her, Ellie resigned from her work. Still she gets calls for help from people who expect her to have all the answers because she's "been there."

PRISCILLA: In one week, she had a call Saturday night, an attempted suicide. [She wasn't home.] She had a call Sunday night, someone in jail. And then a call two days later from the probation officer: "There's this girl who is heavily on narcotics, and ill, and where do I go without calling the police?"

Ellie feels the best she can do with a person in trouble is to "let them tell me. Unless they want to listen, you can't tell them anything. There is nothing you can say. There really isn't. A million people could have talked to me, and I would have gone the same route, y'know?"

And yet, she was willing to give of her time for interviews in the hope that "maybe if some kids who haven't made up their minds can see it all down in front of them, they won't have to try it. I wouldn't want any kid to get messed up in the drug scene."

14

GAPS

WHAT HAVE WE GOT TO OFFER our youngsters that is better than the experience of drugs?

For the believer, the obvious answer is, "The Lord Jesus Christ."

But the problem is, most of our kids have never truly known Christ as a reality in their lives. Their experience in the faith has often been an ineffective (sometimes even offensive) *pattern of Christianity*. It has not often been a redemptive *image of Christ*. Most of our teenagers have been brought up on a Christianity characterized by poorly taught Sunday schools, by admonitions to be "good" (that is, socially acceptable) rather than admonitions to be loving, and by the sting of self-righteous judgmentalism. Often, there has been more emphasis on letter than on spirit, more concern for ritual than for creativity, more self-protectiveness than willingness to risk.

In many cases, Christian has turned his back on Christian as the great issues that divide our land are reflected in our churches. A teen-ager who has been told since his cradle-roll days that "God is love" may find little evidence of that within today's "fellowship" of believers.

Therefore, we must not mouth our belief that Christianity can give that teen a fuller life than drugs do—not unless we are prepared ourselves to do all the things that make the Christian Way work: forgive, go a second mile, suffer persecution for the sake of righteousness, let our light shine before men, love our neighbor as ourself, love our enemies, pray without ceasing, lay up no treasures for ourself on earth, refrain from judging, make love our aim, believe in the life everlasting, love the Lord our God with all our heart, and with all our soul, and with all our mind.

Our kids need to know that all this is more than a way of life. They need to know it is the Way of Life, as taught to us by the one who was himself the way, and the truth, and the life. The way, the truth, and the life—exactly those qualities our kids claim to be searching for through drugs.

So, how do we go about making the person of Christ *real* to our youngsters?

Paul W. Pretzel, Th.D., writing in the *Los Angeles Times*, gives us a direction to explore. He suggests that there is a value gap between young and old in our society. Perhaps this same conflict of values, when put into the context of the church, explains why the Christ of the over-thirties has little reality for our teens.

In an article entitled "Young Drug Users and the 'Value Gap'" (*Los Angeles Times,* March 15, 1970; used by permission of the author), Dr. Pretzel speaks of the "false assumption that there exists a basic sense of values" that both young and old generations hold in common. He goes on to describe it as the false assumption "that all members of our culture hold in common similar life goals, similar concepts of good and evil, and similar basic evaluations of behavior."

Each of the differences listed by Dr. Pretzel has some application for the church.

The first value difference he lists is between pleasure and production. "Young people using drugs defend their use largely on the basis of the pleasure drugs provide. Holding pleasure as an important value, they frequently criticize the older generation for being so obsessed with work and duty that they have lost the ability to be 'turned on' and to accept the multiple pleasures which life has to offer."

We could hardly deny the value of productive work within and by the church. But we are concerned that we have almost denied the validity of pleasure in worship. Dignity has been safeguarded to the degree that some of it has gone sour. It has sometimes turned to joylessness or even to sterility. But a new wind blowing through the church moves us to a celebrative mood. It moves us to affirm the goodness in life, to say, "Yes!" to pleasure and to opportunity and to risk for Christ. It moves us to rejoice because we *know* that the light shines in the darkness and the darkness *has not overcome it!*

This "new wind" is not so new as it is re-newed. It goes back at least as far as King David himself, who was moved to celebrate in worship with great leaping joy. When the ark of God was brought into Jerusalem, "David danced before the LORD with all his might" (II Sam. 6:14).

Those of us who would tend to resist the celebrative mood in our sanctuaries should remember the rest of the story. David's wife Michal "looked out of the window, and saw King David leaping and dancing before the LORD; and she despised him in her heart." After David completed the ceremony, which included a blessing of the people and a communion of sorts, he went home to bless his own household. But when he got there, he and his wife had some strong words, until David finally asserted stoutly, "I will make merry before the LORD." The epilogue to the story is, "And Michal the daughter of Saul had no child to the day of her death." Now whether Michal was childless because she was physiologically barren, or because David had nothing more to do with her, doesn't really matter here. The point is, if today's established church looks on the celebrative mood of her youth as Michal did on David's joy, then the church, too, may find herself without offspring.

We do not suggest that worship should not be dignified. But we do suggest that dignity and solemnity are not synonyms. Clearly, dignity is a quality of the spirit. Solemnity is only a form, and, for some, and at some times, it is not an appropriate form to express the quality of inner joy. That there is dignity of the greatest magnitude in celebration cannot be denied, because the joy of creation is the very essence of our relationship with God.

Listen to the ecstasy of the psalmist as rings forth *his* joy:

Praise the LORD!

. . . . .

Praise him with trumpet sound;
  praise him with lute and harp!
Praise him with timbrel and dance;
  praise him with strings and pipe!
Praise him with sounding cymbals;
  praise him with loud clashing cymbals!
Let everything that breathes praise the LORD!
Praise the LORD!

(Ps. 150.)

The poet is beside himself with utterly joyous worship —the ultimate expression of his love for his Creator. How dare we judge that to be undignified?

Still, we sometimes reflexively reject our youngsters' need to find forms of worship appropriate to their mood of celebration. A remarkable example of this is the automatic disgust many people feel when a guitar is brought into the sanctuary. They feel it is a threat to the dignity of the service. Though the guitar is a very lovely and versatile instrument, there are those for whom the only instrument suitable for worship is the organ. (We wonder what they do with Psalm 150!) And ironically, in another age, the organ was entirely suspect. There is on record an ecclesiastical mandate that the organ shall not be used in church because it is too sensuous an instrument!

So then, if dignity is not a matter of external trappings but of internal feelings, perhaps we mainstream, institutional Christians must bring ourselves to rediscover spontaneity, allow our emotions to show, and become receptive to the dignity in the celebration of life.

Certainly this is true if our youngsters are to discover that the reality *of their feelings* can be congruent to the reality *of worship*.

The second value gap Pretzel speaks of is between experience and achievement. "Young people experimenting with drugs usually place a high value on experience for its own sake. They search for new feelings, new encounters, new insights, and new experiences through varied patterns of dress, drugs, light shows and suspect activities.

"It is an attitude which says that we pass through life but once and that we should taste from many different tables and experience all that there is in life and live it to the fullest."

We do not minimize here the value of achievement. But we do present the idea that our youngsters have the right to find those "new feelings, new encounters, new insights, and new experiences" within the fellowship of the church, or at least within a society that the church should have dramatically influenced.

Dr. Albert Van den Heuvel, former Secretary, Youth Division, World Council of Churches, addressing a small group of American women in Geneva, spoke of the American tendency to "organize away the fragilities of life," such as birth, death, and suffering. That is, generally the really "feeling" experiences of life come to us only in set-apart places. For instance, suffering is attended to by the hospital, or by government welfare bureaus.

In addition to that kind of isolation, we are protected from relating to each other by the pervasiveness of television and by the immovability of our own prejudices.

Can the church change this kind of pattern, so that persons, especially young persons, can experience "all that there is in life and live it to the fullest"? Of course she can, if she will remember that Jesus Christ is in *every experience of our daily living*.

Obviously, we are not suggesting that one should arrange for his next baby to be born in the family patio, or for his great uncle to die in his living room. But the joy and inexpressible wonder of birth, and the sorrow and unfathomable mystery of death are emotions central to the nature of living, and should not be suppressed.

Our teens know joy and sorrow within themselves. But the society that raised them regards those emotions as either too intimate for expression or as something the sophisticated person doesn't need to express. As a result, our youngsters have to choose between what they know of their own feelings and what is expected of their feelings. Those who come to trust their own emotions may seek to explore further their *capability for feeling*.

We believe the church has a better answer than drugs for assisting in that exploration. And certainly a part of that answer lies in exposing kids to the "fragilities of life."

To a degree, the church does this in short-term ways, such as arranging for youths to go Christmas caroling in convalescent homes, or such as planning services for children's hospitals. The ecumenical work camp is another experience many churches and denominations are arranging for their youth. Dr. Van den Heuvel feels that these camps are especially effective ways of providing kids the kind of person-to-person encounter so needed in our society.

But there is yet another—though less dramatic and therefore probably harder—way for Christians to expose kids to the fragilities. We could start by taking seriously the admonition to feed the hungry, welcome the stranger, clothe the naked, visit the sick, visit those in prison. By taking such teaching seriously, we don't mean just contributing money to an organization that will do these things. We mean personally walking the ghetto, offering to babysit for the new neighbors down the block so that they can have a day to get settled, going to the hospital to visit the lonely person, volunteering to do helpful things for the young boys in the local reformatory. Sure, all that is more inconvenient than just writing out a check—but isn't that the point? How else are we going to expose ourselves to the fragilities of life, and therefore build the kind of society in which our kids are also so exposed?

What writing out a check doesn't do is give a sense of interrelating with other persons, of sharing a common humanity, of identifying with another's situation. It's possible that this is the very reason the commune has had such huge appeal for some young persons. The commune promises a sense of community beyond all that kids have experienced before. In fact, Ellie's disappointment with her commune was exactly at this point: the promise was not fulfilled.

Call it the church, or the fellowship, or koinonia, the Christian Way also promises that vital sense of belonging. There is no question that it has often failed too. But the

church does fulfill her promise as each believer responds
to the call to serve his Lord with joy and to love his
neighbor as himself.

The third value difference Dr. Pretzel lists is between
passivity and aggression. "The drug culture places a
high emphasis on passivity, employing terms like 'peace,'
'love,' and 'gentleness.'

"It condemns war, violence, brutality, acquisitiveness
and greed. It prefers passivity to power of any kind, and
sees itself on a high moral plane with this stand. Drugs
are an important part of this value.

"The straight culture places equally high value on
aggression. It uses terms like 'duty,' and 'honor' and talks
about the obligation of every man to fight for what is
right."

We suspect that both ends of this particular value gap
are less than wholesome. Both may be cop-outs. The
passivity of the drug culture appears to be a cop-out
when it becomes a handy and idealistic-sounding excuse
for dropping out of society: that is, for refusing to assume
responsibility so that you do not have to share in the
blame for a society's inadequacies.

Passivity is a cop-out when youngsters claim sole
possession of words such as "love" and "peace." It is a
cop-out when kids are dishonest—or too quick—in their
negative evaluations of their parents' desire to embrace
such virtues.

Passivity is a cop-out when peace and love and gentleness are held up as attitudes achievable best through
drugs. When this happens, youngsters rob themselves of
the victory of "working through" relationships in con-
frontation and creative tension and forgiveness. They also

rob themselves of the victory of growing in their capacity to love.

That the disillusionment of our youth with our society has a valid base cannot be fairly denied by anyone who reads his daily newspaper. When our kids were taught about justice and liberty for all, and about compassion, and about "Thou shalt not kill," somehow or other, they believed us. And now we're stuck with it. But within the drug subculture, the *ideal* may be in danger of fading to only an *idea:* the erosion of energy and motivation provides shallow ground for the nurturing of a complex ideal.

On the other hand, at least within the church, aggression may be a cop-out too. Among the followers of Christ, one sometimes hears more conversation about duty than about love, more about honor than about self-sacrifice, more about country than about Christ. (Red-blooded, stars-and-stripes-type Americans sometimes tend to think of patriotism as the highest good, and tend to use God as a sort of "in case" measure. That's a real cop-out on God!)

Aggression is a cop-out by Christians when it has its focus on self-protectiveness. Those who cannot, for instance, embrace the idea of obeying the teachings of Christ "even at the risk of national security" somehow fail to grasp the significance of a Christ who makes himself totally vulnerable—even unto the cross. This is exactly the point at which passivity and aggression both fail within the church. Neither exposes itself to the rawness of the effort to reconcile; neither pours itself out for the cause of Christ. And yet there is no victory where there is no risk, no insurgence of the love that transforms lives—and transforms societies.

Since neither an insipid passivity nor a nervous aggressiveness seems to be terribly effective for the cause of Christ, Christians ought to explore, then, that other possibility: redeeming vulnerability. That may mean learning what it costs to forgive. It may mean voicing one's compassion to one's bigoted friends. It may mean associating with "those dirty hippies" in order to express the love God has for all his children. Jesus did more than that: He ate with the sinners, remember? He made himself vulnerable to being reviled for the sake of righteousness. "Blessed are those. . ."

For Christians to allow themselves to become so vulnerable would be the "de-cop-outification" of both passivity and aggression. Passivity, if defined as self-sacrifice, is Christlike. And aggression, if defined as actively seeking the most loving way to give of yourself in the struggle for relationship, is also Christlike.

Both, when thus lined up with a redeeming vulnerability, require a thousand times more courage than the old withdrawal passivity, or the old hostile aggressiveness. But that kind of courage is less and less of a problem where there is more and more of a commitment. And the church has her commitment to the person of Jesus Christ, for

> From heaven he came and sought her
> To be his holy bride;
> With his own blood he bought her,
> And for her life he died.

No passivity. No aggressiveness. No cop-out! Just redeeming vulnerability.

Dr. Pretzel's fourth value difference has to do with concepts of time. "The drug culture places a high value on the present; the straight culture sees more value in both the past and the future. The drug culture says the only thing that is really real is the present. . . . The straight culture says that we need both to learn from history and to plan the future, even if this means sacrificing much of the meaning of the moment—an unthinkable bargain for the dedicated drug user."

Theologian Emil Brunner has an interesting theory of the concept of time in relation to the Christian way. He says that faith is the Christian life oriented toward the past, hope is the Christian life oriented toward the future, and love is the Christian way oriented to the present.

Many of today's youngsters would not claim to be specifically Christian. Still, they are known by two descriptive names that Christians ought also to claim: the "love" generation and the "now" generation.

Surely there is necessity for the past and the future, the faith and the hope, in the Christian life. Were this a book for teens we would remind them that God works in and through history, and reveals truth—reveals himself—through men and events in time. We would also discuss the reality of the afterlife, the promise—already kept and demonstrated—of victory over death.

We over-thirties need another reminder: The Christian's individual commitment is not to the past, present, or future, but to the person of Jesus Christ. Nevertheless, the *church's* commitment in time is always to the *present*.

The church is responsible to the past, and she witnesses to the future. But her sphere of influence, her call to teach and to act, is in the *now*. When the church forgets that, she distorts the gospel and alienates not just the young, but all honest persons who have discovered that love is a *present* force that transforms the everyday, moment-to-moment life.

Yet another value gap listed is between content and form. "The straight culture places high value on the content of issues but the drug culture is more apt to be concerned about the form or style by which life is being lived. Where the straight culture sees itself as substantive, valuing facts and content and in-depth penetration, the drug culture pays more attention to flair, form, style, social maneuverability and performance."

The style of celebration is, as already discussed, most pronounced among our youth. Still it is, quite properly, very becoming to the whole Christian fellowship.

Were we to become freer in our expression of celebration, while still maintaining a balance for persons of other worship needs, this form-content gap would be narrowed within the church.

The spirit of ecumenism now rustling through the church will also narrow the gap. Presbyterians are beginning to accept the fact that Catholics are Christians too. And Episcopalians are accepting the fact that Baptists are also Christian. Eventually, we should all become less protective of our own little forms of worship. We will learn that the faith can be expressed in many ways.

And on the other side of the gap, the church *does* have an exciting, vivid, vital content to offer youth. The fact that youth generally considers it dull says a great deal about our church educational system. There are many books about Christian education and ways to make it better. (One of the best of them is Locke Bowman's

Straight Talk About Teaching in Today's Church. The
Westminster Press, 1967.) We do not propose to blue-
print our ideas here, but there is one thing that cannot
be said too often: We need to make our teaching *personal.* Our youngsters need to know that the Christian
way works. And they need to know that it works in *our*
lives. We need to take Christianity out of the insipid
realm of ethics (that is, sending our children to Sunday
school to teach them to be "good"). And we need to put
it back into the realm of salvation (just in case they
sometime fail to be good).

Whether we're talking about salvation, or the resurrection, or the person of Christ, the content of our faith
will not seem dull if our kids feel that it can touch their
lives too. But they won't stand still for canned doctrine,
sweet platitudes, or judgmentalism. They will be convinced only if our witness is personal and honest and
open to their questions.

Another value dichotomy is between risk and restraint.
"Adherents of the drug culture place high value on ex-
citement, risk and adventure; the straight culture prefers
restraint, conservatism, and safety."

Psychologists as well as churchmen have discovered
that there is no love without risk. Not that we flail about
looking for dragons to slay once we have committed
ourselves in love, but that that very commitment is a
risk. We have no guarantee we will be loved back. We
have no guarantee our love will be accepted for what it
is. We have no guarantee the object of our love is really
lovable. Still, once committed to love, that's the risk we
take. Though it is not the kind of physical derring-do

the youth culture demonstrates with its drug roulette, still it is a genuine risk, a "redeeming vulnerability."

Youngsters will understand this if the church will risk boldly. If the local church were to take a strong stand against air pollution, for instance, it would not be much of a risk. Nobody would hiss and boo it for its position, because that's a nice safe topic. But to take a stand on civil rights, or on the Vietnam war, or on MIRV, or on almost any other political issue would be a bolder risk.

There is a sense in which risk is synonymous with involvement. And involvement is a compulsion of love. If the call to the church is to love, the task of the church is to risk. Youngsters can respond to this because it is unhypocritical. It is honest. It places oneself where one's mouth is.

The final value gap listed by Pretzel is between mysticism and intellectualism. "The drug culture is mystical, placing high value on feelings and existential experiences. Truth, they say, is known only by submission to religious experience and the higher mystical life is available for all those willing to accept it.

"The straight culture wants to intellectualize and it values the ability to think and behave rationally above all."

It is true that intellect can sometimes carry us through when feelings fail. "I'm mad at God" (feelings), "but I know that's not going to solve anything" (intellect).

But Christianity is not at its core a *logical* religion. That is, it is not a religion of logic but a religion of faith. And faith has more emotion than it has intellect, and more truth than logic.

Early in Jesus' ministry, a ruler came to him and said, "My daughter has just died, but come and lay your hands on her, and she will live." Now, that's not too logical, is it? But it works.

For some reason many of us straight Christians are afraid to admit having any sort of mystical experience. It's that risk thing again. We're afraid people will think we're strange. Yet so often when a group of Christians begins to share heart-to-heart things, the most wondrous experiences of mysticism are related, such as the "mystic sweet communion with those whose rest is won," or such as sensing the presence of our Lord in a special way. Very often the stories are prefaced with, "I don't tell very many people this, but . . ." because we don't yet trust each other to accept the experience as valid.

Still, if it is valid, somebody ought to let our kids know that they don't need drugs to produce an artificial mysticism. An experience of genuine mysticism happens to ordinary people who aren't saints or prophets or professional mystics on the one hand, or fakers on the other.

Not that our faith should be overbalanced by emotion and mysticism, but that it should be *balanced* by it— pulled back from the danger of becoming merely a thought process. Neither mysticism nor intellectualism alone is worthy of a total commitment. But the church has both and should make no bones about cultivating both aspects of the faith.

Well, then, what do we have to offer kids that is better than the experience of drugs?

For the believer, the answer is still the Lord Jesus Christ. And the believer's problem is still to show the drug-attracted teen that Christ *is* real. But the value gap obstacle is not, after all, unbridgeable. It is bridge-able because one side of the gap is not intrinsically more perfect than the other. As hard as this must seem to each of us, it is true. Christ will become most real to our kids, and to us, too, as we make the effort to reach each other in spite of any value gaps.

15
MIDDLE-CLASS HIPPIE

ELLIE HAS NOW BEEN HOME a full year. She has in that time polished off nearly three years of high school, and she has done so with a very good grade record. This, in spite of the fact that she was also holding down a part-time job at The Gateway much of the year.

As a drama major, she is now beginning her first quarter in a nearby college. Ellie is still on probation, and there is a counselor on campus she sees every week.

In addition to her thirteen units of classes, Ellie is also taking private singing lessons, and this has been especially satisfying for her.

PRISCILLA: We feel that one of the best things about Ellie's college experience is her exposure to a wide variety of personalities. Bob and I are not stressing grades at this point. Right now we think that meeting a wide circle of people is the most important thing that can happen to her, because continuation school provided so narrow a range of acquaintances. She appears to be basically happy in college, and we think she's feeling good about herself, which, of course, is itself very good.

An important aspect of the year has been the strengthened relationship between Ellie and her parents.

ELLIE: It's been about our best year. We are able to talk more—get it out in the open. My mom and I are really close, and I really dig my father too.

PRISCILLA: Ellie has developed a real respect for her father. Also, our whole parent-teen relationship picture has improved in general. We still have our ups and downs, of course. It's not a fairy-tale-come-true sort of thing, but there have been no lasting resentments. I don't believe there have been any differences of opinion within the family that have resulted in any sort of resentment being carried over even into the next day. And that's terribly encouraging. I hope it will be the same with the boys as they grow up. We recognize that surely there are segments of her life we may not know about—after all, she is a freshman in college, and past an age of rigid parental control. If we should sense anything was wrong, we would try to guide, of course. But ultimately the choice is hers.

However, at home, we still have rules. There are chores, curfews, and limitations on the number of nights for dating.

Having to conform to rules again was among the major adjustments Ellie had to make during her first year home.

ELLIE: Also, it was a struggle trying to find out what kinds of crowds I fit into, and trying to keep away from drugs. Now I just tell kids who offer them that I've put down.

Priscilla recalls Ellie's first introduction to straight kids.

PRISCILLA: Ellie attended a church youth retreat within a week or two after she came home. Jim Johnson invited her to play her guitar in the folk worship they were to have. They had a planning meeting for it at our house, and I remember Ellie was pretty scared because a group of church people she didn't even know was coming over.

BOB: It was really her first exposure to normal young people. And it frightened her. But the experience of the retreat they planned that night was a real boost to her. She knew she could be a part of a normal group again, that there could be people within such a group that she could feel in tune with.

Later another pastor in the community invited her to sing and give a personal testimony before his congregation on a Sunday morning. The local newspaper came out the week before with a story headlined "Singer Says She Doesn't Need Dope Anymore." The article went on to tell that Ellie had once been addicted. Even though most of her friends knew all that, she wasn't ready to have it so blatantly publicized. Her first reaction was, "I'm gonna leave the country!" Ultimately she wrote her testimony relating more to the generation gap than to drugs as such.

PRISCILLA: Ellie felt she had something to say in another area besides narcotics, and that it might be of benefit to adults and kids too. She told us she almost gets the feeling sometimes that she is regarded as some kind of freak. And she's not there on the drug scene anymore. As she puts it, she'd just as soon not capitalize on the fact that she'd been there. She'd like to go into a group on her own merit. If the drug thing comes up, she'll not deny it. She might even work it into the conversation herself, but not as the only thing that's important about her: that she was once addicted to narcotics.

Q: What was your reaction to her testimony that Sunday?

PRISCILLA: Mine was just tremendous pride.

BOB: I felt very proud too. I felt that what she was saying showed a tremendous amount of growth on her part. Beforehand, she let me read what she had written, and when I finished I was all choked up. I felt the same way Sunday when I heard her.

It's not surprising that the Bernards were moved by Ellie's testimony. Part of it reads: "Since my return I feel we have really been a family. I feel that I am respected by my parents as an individual with a working mind rather than a mixed-up kid. Their respect has helped me to pull an about-face in the type of person I was and it has brought considerable change to my future."

Ellie offers other parents some suggestions for relating to their returned prodigals.

ELLIE: Parents should realize that when a kid comes

back, he is not the same as when he left. He may still be immature, but he is an adult in many ways. He has had a lot of experiences the parents cannot relate to. And parents should also be willing to hear about those experiences, no matter how hard the stories are to listen to, y'know? The kid has a need to confide, to get some sort of release.

PRISCILLA: It seemed to be important to Ellie to feel that we trusted her to the degree that she could tell us of her life while she was away. So we tried to listen well, even though the temptation was to interrupt with, "I don't want to hear about it—it's too painful," or, "But *why* did you do thus and so?" We learned it is important not to force a youngster to keep admitting his mistake. He's already admitted it by coming back. Also, parents shouldn't keep tossing their own suffering at him. By and large, he wasn't asking them to suffer, he wasn't thinking in terms of the suffering he was going to bring them.

Ellie has a word for youngsters who return, too.

ELLIE: Kids should realize that when they come home, life isn't going to be the same as when they were traveling. They're going to have to bend a bit too. I think I matured a lot this year. I think I learned how to handle responsibility, and I went from being a kid to an adult. Also, I found out what it's like to be middle-class. I don't consider myself a "sosh," but I don't consider myself a righteous freak like I used to be, either. I guess I'm a middle-class hippie.

PRISCILLA: However, Ellie will probably never be typically middle-class in any stereotyped sense. She will always want to explore and to be different.

That may, after all, be her very gift, and in the last analysis the channel through which Ellie will make her creative imprint on those around her.

16

HE IS NOT HOPELESS;
HE IS NOT LOST

Happy, the way that I feel
Knowing everything is real—
The sun will rise
And the moon will glow—
And I close my eyes
And I know what I know.

So sings Ellie in one of her more recent songs, composed when she was "just in a good mood."

Ellie increasingly seems to know what she knows. She knows, for instance, "I don't ever want to get dependent on drugs again." She knows she feels concern for her younger brothers and hopes "they will never have to go through the mess I went through."

She also knows about her parents' anxiety for their sons.

BOB: At this point in time both of the boys express the opinion that they want nothing to do with drugs or with running away. What could happen in their lives in the next five or six years to change this outlook, we just don't know. We're worried.

PRISCILLA: We have wondered what effect the time and attention given to Ellie will have on the boys . . .

BOB: . . . the welcome with open arms, the tears, the love, the new clothes, the medication, and so forth. Are the boys going to say, "Well, what the hell, why shouldn't we try it? Ellie tried it and they didn't do anything to her"? Or, are they going to say, "Gee, Ellie tried it and every time she came home she was sick, and she had to go to juvenile hall, and she was in the psychiatric hospital"?

However, our boys have seen something that should be valuable to them as they think the problem through. They have seen us try to do things as a family of four instead of as a family of five. They have seen that we just could not have the one-hundred-percent good time that we could have had if Ellie had been with us.

We're worried about what they're going to do—but we have great faith in them too.

PRISCILLA: At least we hope that if the boys do make some wrong decisions in the future, they'll know their parents are going to be there to help them all that parents can. They should have the assurance that there's someone they can count on.

And Ellie knows, as no one else knows, how much her parents mean that.

There is no question that Ellie is making a remarkable recovery, and she knows this too. She knows she feels "more comfortable with my way of life now, and with what I'm doing now, than I did before." But she reserves the right to "really dig" a sort of free-spirit intellect among the "middle-class hippies." "Someday I want my own pad with millions of records and millions of books."

Ellie knows she is full of the kind of dreams every seventeen-year-old lives on. She wants marriage and kids, she wants fame as a singer, she wants to travel, and she's looking forward to being on her own. And, considering the depth of the person she is, and considering her singing voice, and her past record of travel, and her sense of self-sufficiency, she should know it is not likely that any of these dreams will have to go unfulfilled.

Ellie knows that one of the most difficult things to deal with within herself this year has been "my impatience—with myself and my age. I'd like to be eighteen, and on my own, and supporting myself." She recognizes that this is not an unnatural need, especially in view of already having been on her own for the better part of two years. "And when I finally do settle down somewhere, I know it will be someplace close to nature —like in the mountains."

Much of Ellie's current poetry reflects her sensitivity to nature:

> And when I go to the sea
> I am a shell
> Alone in myself
> but welcoming the visiting waves
> That smooth my skin.

One important thing Ellie may not yet know is who Ellie really is. Mr. Johnson says, "I don't really think she has got that one solved yet." She is, after all, only now seventeen years old. How many seventeen-year-olds are already clear about the direction of their lives? Ellie has a lot of exploring of her own creative selfhood to do before she'll be ready to commit herself to any pattern of life.

MR. JOHNSON: Being a human being, especially a very complex human being, she can expect to have more problems. I really think that she is over the hump on drugs, though.

Ellie's parents also feel that her drug experience is of the past. They have genuine hopefulness for her future.

PRISCILLA: We know now that we can ultimately believe in each of our children, and in ourselves too. This does not mean there may be no heartbreak. But it does mean we do not have to live with it as a way of life. There is hope.

The quality of this hope is suggested in the poem "The Concert" by Edna St. Vincent Millay. Though it is highly unlikely that the poet had the teen struggle in mind when she wrote it, parts of the poem sound like today's youngster talking to today's parent.

No, I will go alone.
I will come back when it's over.
Yes, of course I love you.
No, it will not be long.

. . . .

Come now, be content.
I will come back to you, I swear I will;
And you will know me still.
I shall be only a little taller
Than when I went.

So, then, what of you and of your child, whom you yearn to hold so close to you?

He will go off to his "concert" alone.
But he *will* come back when it's over!
Yes, of course, he loves you!
No, it will not be nearly so long as it would seem
    from here.

Come now, though you cannot be content, be con-
    soled.
He will come back to you, we swear he will.
And you will know him still.
He will be, if you will but affirm it, a little taller
    than when he went.

It *is* possible, even amidst the discord of his con-
    cert, for him to hear a quieter call.
He is *not* hopeless!
He is *not* lost!
He *is* able, even yet, to make it through!

17
EVEN
THE HARD-CORE KIDS

IT IS STEADFASTLY TRUE that most youngsters will choose to disentangle themselves from their muck, when they have suffered enough and learned enough from their suffering.

But what about hard-core cases? What about the youngster who is irrevocably committed to crime and drugs and ugliness as a way of life? or the youngster whose mental capacities have been seriously and permanently impaired by drugs? Is there valid reason for parents to hold hope for these apparently hopeless children?

Strongly, *yes!*

Obviously, we're not dealing with a cloying, untrue, "everything will turn out okay and be just like it was before" kind of hope. But we *are* dealing with a no-nonsense kind of hope that springs from the reality of two potent, vibrant miracles: conversion and healing.

In this point in time there is no dearth of examples of youngsters committed to drugs and ugliness. The Tate and LaBianca murders, for instance, have received a great deal of publicity since they took place in 1969. The youngsters accused of that nightmare—which seems so very grotesque, so fantasylike, so evil—represent the kind of hard-core youngster who has chosen the ugly life.

Part of the horror, part of that which the mind keeps trying to reject, is the fact that some of those accused were young, attractive girls, girls from broken, but not necessarily unwholesome, homes. Somehow, it felt like the loss of innocence from our society as a whole.

How terribly the experience must have devastated the youngsters' parents! "Losing" a child in this manner must surely be the most cruel way of all.

It would be unrealistic drivel to try to comfort by saying, "It will all work out all right." In practical terms, in terms of coming through unscarred, there is no return. The design of those youngsters' lives has of course been drastically altered by their involvement in drugs.

But the point is, for them, and for a thousand other kids gone "bad," religious conversion is still the most live of live possibilities. As remote and unreal and impossible as it may seem, conversion can and *often* does occur, no matter how terrible the crime, no matter how cynical the criminal. If we do not believe this, we really do not have very much confidence in the saving power of Jesus Christ.

The Spirit of Christ does seem to be moving kids in

many varied ways. For instance, the winds of revival
have been blowing with uncanny effectiveness across our
college campuses. All those stories of riots, free love,
and drug use on our campuses are undoubtedly true.
But they pale in significance beside the monumental fact
of the conversion experience that is sweeping the colleges of our nation (but getting no major headlines).

This "revival," if you will, is sometimes called the
Asbury College Revival. It would appear that Asbury
College in Wilmore, Kentucky, is being used by the
Holy Spirit as a focal point for a rebirth, a quickening,
a new impulse of the life in Christ.

It appears to have begun on February 3, 1970. On that
morning, when students gathered for their regular ten
o'clock chapel service, several of them quietly told of
the change they had felt in their lives since they had
begun spending a part of each day in prayer and in
reading Scripture.

It was as if someone had peeled off a collective mask,
exposing the needs of the students present. One youngster after another got up to confess, to forgive, to praise,
to pray, to testify to feeling cleansed.

Twenty-four hours later the service was still going on,
and classes had been recessed. By Wednesday, most of
the thousand students at the college had come to speak
of their faith. And word of the service had spread to the
surrounding communities. The service continued nonstop
for 180 hours—more than a week.

Estimates vary of the number of persons who were
caught up in that "moment" of conversion. Some say
there were 12,000; others say 16,000. Students, faculty,
townspeople, laymen, and even passing travelers were
among them.

Sparks from that fire have very quickly ignited schools all over the country, as Asbury has been swamped with pleas to "come and tell us what is happening there."

Within a few months, at least seven hundred Asbury students went out to tell the story. Close to sixty colleges and churches in sixteen states experienced the same irresistible movement of the Spirit by the end of March, and there have been many more since then.

Probably the most telling element of this movement of the Spirit is that it is just that. It was not planned by man. No one intended for it to happen. It was not centered on the charisma of any human personality.

Has it reached the drug-attracted teen? Yes. In fact, the report is that some kids are meeting for Bible study in places they had formerly reserved for "doping."

From Anderson, Indiana, came this loving report: "Among those converted this weekend was a mainliner. He truly has the victory in the Lord Jesus Christ. Good Christian people are loving him and praying for him. Join us in continuing prayer for him."

Youngsters not in college are also being caught up by the Holy Spirit: the dropouts, the dopers in high school, the street people, the youngsters who are trying to find themselves amid drugs and pads and weirdo clothes. Unexpectedly, a very fundamentalist heaven-and-hell brand of Christianity has turned many kids of this life-style off the stuff and on to God. They sometimes call themselves Jesus freaks and they use phrases like "Turn on with Jesus" and "Working for Jesus is like wow!" Such terms may be offensive to the theologically proper creedal advocate, but on the other hand, "Very God of Very God" just doesn't cut it with the dopers. "Christ is a good trip" apparently communicates enough of the good news to the spiritually hungry hippie type to turn him to the better Way. "You can rap with God" may not sound very elegant, but one cannot deny that the thought behind it is basic to our faith. Nor can we deny that such fundamentalism, narrow and incomplete and crude as it may seem, is blowing clean air through the drugged atmosphere of San Francisco's former hippie culture, and through rural whistle-stops like Nuevo, California, and through a hundred other places where drugs have had their hold.

The conversion experience is a huge mystery. What is it that causes us to yield up the self in us and become new persons?

Writer Starr Daily, whose conversion of the soul occurred as he lay on the floor in the solitary confinement pit of a prison, says: "In one moment I was a confirmed criminal. In the next I was healed. . . . I cannot explain the mystery of it. I only know that it was an inner experience of some sort, a huge and different experience." (Starr Daily, *Release*; Harper & Brothers, 1942.)

The *unfathomableness* of what happens in the conversion experience does not in any sense detract from the fact that something real, so real, *does* happen to persons, and they are never the same persons again.

Certainly the apostle Paul is the classic example.

Shortly after the death of Christ, those who were his followers came under a terrible persecution. They were dragged from their homes in heartbreaking ruthlessness, and thrown into prison. One of the most severe of the punishers was a young Jew who received official permission to go as far as Damascus from Jerusalem to "beat the bushes" looking for Christians.

As he came near the city, this angry young man got

jolted to his knees with the sudden drama of his encounter with Christ. There was great light and the sound of a voice, and from it all a greatly shaken Paul emerged to become the most intense proclaimer of the good news that history has ever recorded.

Does all this seem too long ago and too dramatic to hold much comfort for the grieving parent of today? Then listen to the clear, straightforward, honest words of a nineteen-year-old former member of the Hell's Angels Motorcycle Club. Members of Hell's Angels are known for their terrorizing of towns, their propensity toward unprovoked violence, their sexual promiscuities, their utter disregard for law.

The following was extracted from a presentation the young man made before an assembly sponsored by Campus Crusade for Christ:

Ex-Hell's Angel: I was way up there in the top ranks in the Hell's Angels Club in my area. My club name was Psycho, and I had run with the Angels since I was about thirteen years old. My two "brothers" that I grew up with —they were sixteen and I was about thirteen—were Beast and Deacon. I grew up at the top, and naturally since I grew up at the top, I became the top. I got carried away. I found that my life that I had started and thought I could control, controlled me. When I was around thirteen, I started using drugs. Just small drugs: pot, uppers, downers. I started joy poppin' on heroin at fourteen. All my friends would use heroin, and then what was left over on the cotton I'd clean out and use myself. When I was fifteen and sixteen years old, I was going on to heavier things, not on heroin so much as on cocaine here and there. I was smoking a lot more pot, I was dropping a lot more uppers, and a lot more downers, and I was shootin' 'em, and I was just being carried away. Like I said, my life got a hold of me. It got worse and worse. I turned seventeen, then eighteen. All of a sudden then I shot heroin, mainline. Not enough people have mainlined on heroin and come off of it alive to tell people how bad it is. How really *bad* that is. People don't realize until they try it what pain is and what agony is. And I tell you there is no pain or agony on this earth that matches up to cold-turkey heroin. I overdosed one day. I shot a hundred and fifty bucks worth of heroin. I was averaging fifty dollars a day, but I couldn't get enough that day. I was trying to kill myself. A hundred and fifty bucks. You think about that! I crawled into a big square, metal trash can, and for four days I laid in there. Whatever imaginable thing you can think of happened to me in those four days. I hallucinated. I was in pain. I bled. I vomited. Whatever you can name, it was happening to me, and it was all over me at the bottom of that garbage. I lived right in the middle of hell.

Like I say, I mainlined on fifty dollars of drugs a day. Then, one day I went to a Billy Graham Crusade. I had been mainlining for a couple of months, so I had a pretty substantial habit. A pretty set habit. It wasn't easy to give up. Nobody that I know has ever given up smack [heroin] and stayed off of it. But I went to the Billy Graham Crusade and I sat there for four days. The first day I decided to come off of drugs by myself. The second day I started to change my mind. The third day I was rolling around out there in the big grass field, because of the pain I was going through. The fourth day I couldn't take it anymore.

There is nothing on this earth that I hadn't done, and nothing on this earth that I hadn't tried. Nothin' works. *Nothin'* works! You're *lost!*

Finally I broke down. I said, "Jesus Christ, I've lived a lousy life. But now if you want me, you take me." And I asked him to come in.

That simple little thing of asking him to come into my heart gave me a relaxation. The pain stopped, and I haven't had a wantin' for heroin since. And I never will. I came off of heroin just by asking Jesus Christ to be my Lord and Savior. He's real. He's *real!*

I've got "brothers." Beast? He's a Christian. Deacon? He's becoming an ordained minister. I'm Psycho, I'm a Christian, and I tell you right now there are close to five hundred Angels that are Christian, and we're starting a new club. It's called Angels for Christ. [*Laughter and applause from audience.*] I tell you, Jesus is working; 'Cause not one of us really had anything to do with another one's help! Jesus took all of us just about the same time. We all found Christ, and then we all got together. But Jesus really worked heavy on that! When he gets to you, you can see your life going straight up!

"Straight up" for this young man includes working on a church staff, witnessing to other youth.

Psycho was asked, "Whatever got you to go to a Billy Graham Crusade in the first place?"

To which he responded: "It was my mother. She'd been praying for me for seven years, trying to get me to straighten up. Seven years! Finally, she talked me into going to that Crusade with her."

Parents whose prayers for their children sometimes

seem so futile may feel a deeply personal response to that answer.

That five hundred former Hell's Angels are now Christian may be a fairly conservative guess. And there are other Christian motorcycle clubs besides Angels for Christ. Christ Patrol, for instance, with at least twenty clubs across the country, counts many among its members who have been in serious trouble with the law.

Clearly, then, conversion is not an isolated or remote experience. It is a *common* experience, a legitimate hope, the promise of the Holy Spirit. And, it's happening *today,* even to the *most* hopeless of cases.

Obviously, when a youngster becomes committed to the Christian Way, he will still have to suffer the consequences of any serious crimes he may have previously committed. But it is critically important for parents to understand that even the *most utterly hopeless* youngster has not traveled so far as to be out of the reach of a loving Lord: "Whither shall I flee from thy presence? If I ascend into heaven, thou art there. If I make my bed in hell, thou art there!"

For the youngster who is committed to drugs as a way of life, the miracle of conversion, then, is certainly one hope to which parents have every right to cling.

But parents of the youngster whose mind has been damaged by chemicals may feel his situation is different, and beyond all hope.

But there *is* hope: the same Lord who changes minds also *heals* minds.

A huge power for healing, for making whole, for reconciling flesh and mind and spirit, is an integral part of our New Testament heritage. And it is available to us at the level of our everyday lives.

Somehow, those of us who have been brought up in the major Protestant denominations are not always entirely comfortable with that idea. In the main we have distrusted the healing experience. We have come close to scoffing at the Lourdes of our Roman Catholic brothers, and we have come close to sneering at the Oral Robertses and Brother Allens and Kathryn Kuhlmans of our more evangelical brothers. Yet over and over and over again, Jesus demonstrated the integrity of the healing experience. Healing is inseparably entwined with his whole mission. In fact, when John the Baptist sent a messenger to ask if Jesus were really the Messiah, Jesus answered by comparing the Old Testament expectation of the Messiah against his own ministry: "Go back and tell John what you have seen and heard: the blind can see, the lame can walk, the lepers are made clean, the deaf can hear, the dead are raised to life, and the Good News is preached to the poor" (Luke 7:22, Today's English Version; American Bible Society, 1966).

Healing and resurrection and the good news of God's love: this is the reconciling work of the Messiah.

Because healing makes things whole, it is, in the New Testament, a sort of acted symbol of the reconciliation for which both the Lord and his people yearned. Resurrection is the proof of that reconciliation, and proclaiming the good news is a response to it.

Christ not only used his power to heal continuously; he gave that power to his followers. He "called the twelve disciples together and gave them power and authority to drive out all demons and cure diseases. Then he sent them out to preach the Kingdom of God and to heal the sick." In this context, this is the mission of the church: to preach and to heal—to proclaim that God wants us reconciled to him, and to demonstrate a kind of reconciliation, a making of persons whole.

Many of the incidents of healing recorded in the New Testament are healings of deranged persons. Jesus' healing of the Gerasene demoniac is one instance; Paul's healing of the slave girl at Philippi is another. Why, then, are we reluctant to believe that such healing can happen to the drug-damaged teen?

Healing as an acted symbol was a very direct way for Christ to communicate the love and compassion of the Father. It is no less direct today—*and no less profoundly real.*

On the one hand, healing happens directly through our prayer. (That's the point of our prayer, isn't it? Then let's have a little faith in it.) And on the other hand, healing takes place as Christ chooses to work through someone who has a special gift for healing.

The problem, of course, is to sort out the genuine healing experience from the experience produced by some sort of hysteria. One can, for instance, evaluate the mass healer–evangelists only according to one's own sense of reality and propriety. Often there is a great deal of showmanship that one must wade through to see what is or isn't happening. The key is to not lump the mass healers into one category of either good or bad, but to keep an open mind—in both directions.

Unfortunately, the mass evangelists probably overshadow the quieter healers by faith, of whom there may be a surprising number in local congregations. (Unfortunately, in many congregations of the "respectable" ilk, the healing power is one of those things people seem to share only in the "safeness" of intimate fellowship.)

In recent years, several devoted and unassuming persons who are not mass evangelists have come to prominence because of their remarkable healing works. Two of them are Olga and Ambrose Worrall. Their personal story, *The Gift of Healing*, reads like a novel and opens up new channels for belief in this reality called healing. Another is Agnes Sanford, who was herself healed of acute depression by the healing touch of a concerned minister. She subsequently began exploring the healing experience. It has since been given to her to heal others of both mental and physical illnesses. At least two of her books, *The Healing Gifts of the Spirit* and *The Healing Light,* aim at sharing this gift with others.

The Worralls are "sensitives" in the parapsychological sense of the word. Mrs. Sanford is not. But the common element among them, the thing that makes them significant here, is that in all other ways these are ordinary persons. They have not sought fame. They have not capitalized on their gifts. They are not rich or famous or glamorous or dramatic. They do not hold outlandish or unusual jobs: Mrs. Sanford, before her marriage, was a teacher. Ambrose Worrall is consultant to an industrial corporation. Olga Worrall, prior to becoming director of a healing clinic, was "just" a housewife. All of which is exactly our point: the gifts of the Spirit, including the gift of healing, are given to persons just like the rest of us. The chances are excellent that somewhere in any community there are those who have not blown trumpets but who may be very effective channels for the healing desire of Christ.

To convince the reader of the reality, and availability, and appropriateness of the healing experience to the Christian community is our only aim here. We plead with those we have not convinced to at least read such books as we have mentioned lest the door be closed to what may be the hope of their youngster's well-being. For we *are* convinced: a son or daughter's mind *may* be called back, even from drug damage. We are convinced because we know that wholeness is the intent and purpose and hope of a loving Christ for that youngster.

SUMMARY

Two little caterpillars inching their way through the grass paused to watch a butterfly flutter over them. One caterpillar turned to the other and said, "You'll never get me up in one of those things!"

Most little caterpillars who look upon the butterfly may not recognize that it is their own destiny they are viewing. But they will experience metamorphosis anyway! That is the way of God's nature.

Most young drug addicts who look upon the resurrection, upon the ultimate healing and transforming act of Christ, may not see that as their own destiny either. But they too are able to experience metamorphosis. That is the way of God's *healing*.

And some young drug addicts who look upon the resurrection *are* able to see in it their own already fulfilled hope for reconciliation. And they will leap to their meta-morphosis! That is the way of God's *conversion*.

You who are parents of drug-attracted teens, turn your eyes upon the butterfly, upon the resurrection. And know that your youngster is never, not ever, without the hope of Christ.